2 **Workbook**

Spelling, Punctuation and Grammar

GET IT RIGHT

Frank Danes

Jill Carter

OXFORD
UNIVERSITY PRESS

Contents

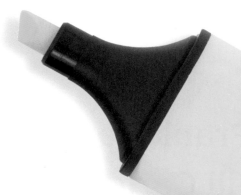

Introduction

How this workbook will help you

This workbook aims to provide you with an accessible introduction to the basics of spelling, punctuation and grammar. The workbook focuses on what you need to know to write fluently and accurately through supportive teaching text and a range of targeted activities.

How this workbook is structured

The workbook is split into three chapters, covering spelling, punctuation and grammar. Each topic in the chapters includes key teaching information and explanation, followed by a range of structured activities to test your understanding.

The workbook also has a clear focus on spelling, punctuation and grammar in context. Selected topics across the workbook feature an 'in context' spread; these spreads include a carefully-selected source text extract and a range of activities that ask you to consider how and why the author has used a particular technique for effect.

Exploring new texts

This workbook introduces you to a range of fiction and non-fiction texts from different historical periods (from the 19th, 20th and 21st centuries), which will help to prepare you for the type of texts you will encounter throughout your English studies.

Which features are included?

The workbook offers a range of varied activities to test your understanding of all the spelling, punctuation and grammar topics, as well as tasks that challenge you to explore the effects of specific grammatical choices in source text extracts. There are spaces to write your answers throughout.

Throughout this workbook, you will find 'Tips' to help support your understanding of difficult concepts, along with a 'Find out more' feature that will direct you to other related topics in the workbook.

For ease of reference, there is also a complete glossary at the end of the workbook that explains all of the relevant spelling, punctuation and grammar terms used throughout the book.

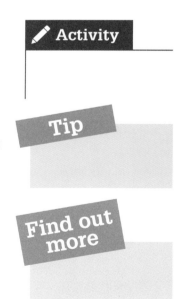

Activity

Tip

Find out more

1 Nouns

What are nouns?

A noun names a person, place, idea or thing.

Bobby	New York	rage
weather	grass	table

How do they work?

Nouns can be divided into concrete nouns and abstract nouns. They can also be divided into countable and uncountable nouns.

Concrete and abstract nouns

A concrete noun is a noun that can be experienced physically so it can either be seen, touched, heard, smelt or tasted.

rain	tree	cake	door

An abstract noun is a noun that cannot be physically experienced. Abstract nouns can include emotions, ideas, processes or states of being.

development	adolescence	dream	evil	joy

Countable and uncountable nouns

A countable noun is a noun that you can count and turn into a plural, usually by adding an **–s** to the singular noun:

one **spaceship**	→	thirty-two **spaceships**
one **dustbin**	→	four million **dustbins**

An uncountable noun is a noun that cannot be made into a plural.

bread	information	rice	music
weather	accommodation	luggage	happiness

You can ask for more or less bread or rice, but you can't ask for two bread or twenty rice. Uncountable nouns are sometimes called mass nouns.

Concrete is a concrete noun!

Tip

Nouns can also be divided into proper and common nouns. Proper nouns start with a capital letter because they name very specific people, places or things, e.g. William, Italy, Mount Everest.

✏ Activity 1

Fill in the gaps in the text below. Make sure you include at least two uncountable nouns.

The most interesting _thing_ in the safari park was the _giraffe_.
I always experienced a tremendous sense of _awe_ when I gazed at it. This
was only equalled by the extraordinary _pleasure_ I felt when I paused to watch the
zebras. "Dad," I said, "can I feed it some _rice_?"

/6

✏ Activity 2

a) Circle all of the concrete nouns in the paragraph below. There are eight concrete nouns in total.

b) Now underline the all of the abstract nouns in the paragraph. There are eight abstract nouns in total.

Tucked up in her bed, her dreams were full of contentment and satisfaction. She no longer worried about packing her bag with the correct schoolbooks every morning. She lived in a story in which she rode a unicorn, slew the dragon and was crowned queen. She dispensed justice wisely, ensuring that good reigned and evil was punished. A smile played over her face as she slept.

/16

✏ Activity 3

Are the nouns listed below countable or uncountable? Tick the correct box in the table below.

Nouns	Countable noun	Uncountable noun
a) wall	✓	
b) river	✓	
c) knowledge		✓
d) country	✓	
e) safety		✓
f) evidence	✓	
g) paint	✓	

/7

2 Noun phrases

What are noun phrases?

A noun phrase is a phrase that has a noun as its key word or head word. All the other words in the noun phrase add extra detail about the noun. An example of a noun phrase is 'a jar of honey'.

How do they work?

Noun phrases can be put together like this:

Take a noun: **chocolate**

↓

Add a determiner: **the** chocolate

↓

Add an adjective to modify the noun: the **scrumptious** chocolate

Noun phrases can be made up of just a noun and a determiner, for example 'my books' or they can be much longer, such as the examples underlined in the sentences below. Noun phrases never contain a verb.

The noun phrases in the sentences below have been underlined in blue. The head words are in green.

head word / noun phrase

A **spoonful** of sugar helps the medicine go down.

head word / noun phrase

I wish my older **brother** wasn't so intelligent.

head word / noun phrase

I should never have sent you to see that ridiculous **film**.

Note that words in a noun phrase can come both before and after the head word. A very long noun phrase is known as an expanded noun phrase. In the example below, the expanded noun phrase is underlined and the head word is in green.

My favourite character is the ever-greedy but much-loved fictional **caterpillar** in that children's book.

Find out more

There is more about determiners on page 32.

✏ Activity 1

Circle the head word in each noun phrase below.

a) the evergreen trees

b) a threadbare but favourite soft toy

c) an elderly man with a white stick

d) all the students in the gold team

e) some people with extraordinary powers

/5

✏ Activity 2

Underline the noun phrases in the following sentences and circle the head words. The first one has been done for you.

Note that some sentences contain more than one noun phrase.

a) The most recent scientific (research) indicates that dolphins can talk.

b) They had to queue before they could see the latest *Star Wars* film.

c) She guided the boat into the mouth of the harbour.

d) The Spanish teacher wore flamboyant dresses.

e) My beautiful puppy is actually very hard to train.

f) Spike knew he had to venture down the dark alley.

g) Just add a splash of milk, please.

/16

✏ Activity 3

**Write four noun phrases using the nouns below as head words.
At least one should be an expanded noun phrase.**

Note: some of these words can also be used as verbs – make sure you use them as nouns in your phrases!

celebrity   parachute   bully   match

/4

7

Noun phrases in context

Extract from *Silas Marner* by George Eliot, published 1861

In this extract, a small girl has mysteriously appeared in the cottage of a lonely weaver, Silas Marner, and he is trying to look after her.

He had plenty to do through the next hour. The porridge, sweetened with some dry brown sugar from an old store which he had **refrained from** using for himself, stopped the cries of the little one, and made her lift her blue eyes with a wide quiet gaze at Silas, as he put the spoon into her mouth. Presently she slipped from his knee

5 and began to toddle about, but with a pretty stagger that made Silas jump up and follow her lest she should fall against anything that would hurt her. But she only fell in a sitting **posture** on the ground, and began to pull at her boots, looking up at him with a crying face as if the boots hurt her. He took her on his knee again, but it was some time before it occurred to Silas's dull **bachelor** mind that the wet boots were the

10 grievance, pressing on her warm ankles. He got them off with difficulty, and baby was at once happily occupied with the primary mystery of her own toes, inviting Silas, with much chuckling, to consider the mystery too. But the wet boots had at last suggested to Silas that the child had been walking on the snow, and this roused him from his entire **oblivion** of any ordinary means by which it [the little girl] could have entered

15 or been brought into his house. Under the prompting of this new idea, and without waiting to form **conjectures**, he raised the child in his arms, and went to the door.

refrained from – resisted
posture – position
bachelor – unmarried man

oblivion – a state of a lack of awareness
conjectures – guesses

✏ Activity 1 Understanding the text

a) What kind of food does Silas decide to feed the toddler?

----

b) What is he concerned about once she is moving around the room?

----

c) What is bothering the little girl?

----

d) Why does Silas decide to go to the door?

Activity 2 Exploring the writer's technique

a) Re-read the following sentence:

The porridge, sweetened with some dry brown sugar from an old store which ...ed from using for himself, stopped the cries of the little one, and ...er blue eyes with a wide quiet gaze at Silas, as he put the spoon ...n.

...rases using the table below:

describes	Dry brown sugar ✓
describes	Old store ✓
describes	Blue eyes ✓
describes ...s at Silas	with a wide quiet gaze ✓

...mples of noun phrases in the text. Remember a noun phrase ... a noun.

✗ dull bachelor mind

...ge, sweetened ✗ a crying face

...r use certain noun phrases in this text? Choose three noun phrases you ...y interesting and effective in this extract. Discuss why they are effective ...s passage. You could use some of the following effects to help you:

...us to imagine | generate a more specific idea | create a more vivid image

... uses certain noun phrases in this text ... a more vivid image ✓ For example ...ooks at Silas "with a wide quiet gaze". ... us to understand that she is ...ith the porridge ✓ Another effective ... "dry brown sugar", from this we can *

* deduce that the bachelor is most likely to be poor. "old store" is a good phrase to use too, because it suggests he bought it a long time ago and he is saving it for as long as possible as he is poor.

Activity 3 Try it yourself

On a separate piece of paper, write a paragraph describing a small child you know. Use noun phrases to add detail and create a vivid image of the child. You could include references to:

- their movements
- their voice
- their facial expressions.

3 Pronouns

What are pronouns?

A pronoun is a word that can be used instead of a noun or noun phrase.

How do they work?

There are many types of pronouns, including personal pronouns, which refer to a person, animal or thing (**I**, **you**, **she**, **he**, **it**, **we**, **they**) and possessive pronouns, which refer to things that are owned (**mine**, **yours**, **hers**, **his**, **its**, **ours**, **theirs**).

The main focus of this unit is demonstrative pronouns and relative pronouns.

Demonstrative pronouns

A demonstrative pronoun shows whether something or someone is near or further away. The following are all demonstrative pronouns:

this	that	these	those

demonstrative pronouns that show that someone or something is close by
→ **This** is my friend Sven.
→ **These** are my new pet vultures.

demonstrative pronouns that show that someone or something is further away
→ **That** is my phone.
→ **Those** are the shoes I'm saving up for.

Relative pronouns

A relative pronoun starts a relative clause, which gives more information about a noun.

The following are all relative pronouns:

which	that	who	whom	whose

relative pronoun
I have completely forgotten the book <u>that</u> I read last week. — relative clause

relative pronoun
Steve, <u>whose</u> parents live in the prettiest area of town,</u> is a most suitable fiancé for you. — relative clause

Find out more

There is more about nouns on page 4.

Tip

Who or whom? Use the pronoun 'who' when it is the subject of a verb, e.g. 'Who has eaten all the sandwiches?'. Use 'whom' when it is the object of a verb or before a preposition, e.g. 'the girl whom I saw', 'the soldier to whom I gave the flag'.

Find out more

There is more about relative clauses on page 38.

Activity 1

Circle the eight pronouns in the extract from the script below. Remember to look for all types of pronouns, not just demonstrative and relative.

The Shadow:	The Time Destructor is *mine*, for ever!
Petronella:	No, *it* is *ours!*
Dom:	*This* is ridiculous. *It's* just a lump of metal.
The Shadow:	*You* fool. The 'lump of metal', *which* *I* am standing on, is the key to the universe!

8 /8

Activity 2

Add the correct relative pronoun to the following sentences:

a) It was Gran ___who___ told us the answer in the end.

b) It was the dentist ___whose___ tropical fish won the award.

c) I knew it was someone important ___that___ I was speaking to.

d) Of the three guards, there was one ___who___ told you the secret password.

e) Millie, ___who___ was very bored with the lesson, put her head on the desk and snored.

5 /5

Activity 3

Imagine a time in the future. You are taking a friend back to your current house or the school you go to now. Write a short paragraph on separate paper describing:

- what is close to you, using the demonstrative pronouns *this* and *these*

- what is further away from you, using the demonstrative pronouns *that* and *those*.

/6

Tip

Use a form of the verb 'to be' after these demonstrative pronouns:

This is the place where…

Those were the…

That was where…

Verbs: phrasal verbs and the imperative form

What are verbs?

A verb is a word that identifies a thought, feeling or action. It can describe physical actions or thoughts and feelings.

verbs

I **write** songs, **shop** for clothes and **think** about friends.

Find out more

There is more about subject and verb agreement on page 20.

How do they work?

The base form of the verb is called the infinitive. It often (but not always) has the word 'to' in front of it.

to open   to drink   to write

Verbs change depending on who is doing the action: the subject of the verb.

I open   **she** opens   **they** open

subject

Phrasal verbs

A phrasal verb is an expression that includes at least two words, including a verb plus a preposition and/or an adverb.

The individual words in a phrasal verb do not have their usual meaning, but together make a new meaning.

look after   back down   wash up

verb   preposition

Please **look after** your beautiful cat costume.

phrasal verb meaning 'take care of'

Don't **mess about** when you are **washing up**!

Imperative form

The word 'imperative' means something that must be done. The imperative form of a verb tells someone to do something as an instruction or a command.

The imperative usually has no subject but can have an object, as in two of the examples below.

Stop!   **Wash** the dishes.   **Watch** the television.

imperatives

> **Tip**
>
> Some imperatives are made up of phrasal verbs. For example, 'Get out!' and 'Keep off!'.

Activity 1

The second word has been left out of each phrasal verb below. Write the correct words in the spaces.

Ian finds it very difficult to keep _____ with classwork, mainly because he insists on messing _____ and showing _____ rather than concentrating. He even nods _____ and sleeps if he thinks the lesson is boring. I am no longer prepared to put _____ with his behaviour: I am therefore resigning and taking _____ an easier profession, like lion taming.

/6

Activity 2

Read the following sentences carefully and then add a suitable imperative in each space. The first example has been completed for you.

a) Take care! Unauthorised use of the airlock may result in oxygen loss.

b) _____ your name and the date at the top of the exam paper.

c) _____ the onions and put them in the frying pan.

d) _____ from me! How dare you disturb me at this time?

/3

Activity 3

Underline the phrasal verbs and circle the imperatives in the following sentences. Note that some phrasal verbs may also be imperatives.

a) Be quiet! If you don't stop messing about, I shall do something drastic.

b) Leave me alone. I have to wash up all these dirty dishes.

c) Look after the baby dinosaurs carefully. They have sharp teeth. Watch out!

/8

Phrasal verbs and the imperative form in context

Extract from the Royal National Lifeboats Institution (RNLI) website

In this extract, the RNLI gives some advice about safety on the beach.

Flags

If the beach you're at is not lifeguarded, please take extra care if you are going into the water. If lifeguards are on patrol, then you'll need to know your flags:

5 <u>Red and yellow flags:</u> Lifeguarded area. Safest area to swim, bodyboard and use **inflatables**.

<u>Black and white chequered flags:</u> For surfboards, stand-up paddleboards, kayaks and other non-powered craft. Launch and recovery area for kitesurfers and windsurfers. Never swim or bodyboard here.

<u>Red flag:</u> Danger! Never go in the water under any circumstances when the red flag
10 is flying.

<u>Orange **windsock**:</u> Indicates offshore or strong wind conditions. Never use inflatables when the windsock is flying.

Sun safety

Sunburn can ruin your holiday and increase the risk of skin cancer in later life.
15 According to our friends at the Karen Clifford Skin Cancer Charity Skcin, we experience over half our lifetime's exposure to the sun before we reach the age of 21.

So please, keep safe this summer and follow the five Ss of sun safety:

- Sunscreen – slop on **SPF** 30+ broad-spectrum waterproof sunscreen every 2 hours

- Sun hat – slap on a broad-brimmed hat that shades your face, neck and ears

20 - Sunglasses – wear wrap-around sunglasses with UV protection to shield your eyes

- Shoulders – slip on a T-shirt or **UV** protective suit for children and remember to keep your shoulders covered

- Shade – seek shade, particularly during the hottest time of the day between 11am and 3pm when UV penetration is at its strongest.

inflatables equipment that can be filled with air, e.g. small boats

windsock a conical tube that indicates wind direction and speed

SPF sun protection factor

UV ultraviolet

✏ **Activity 1** | **Understanding the text**

a) What kind of flag indicates that you should never go in the water? -

b) What is used to indicate wind conditions? -

c) Why is sunburn dangerous? Give two reasons.

- -

- -

✏ **Activity 2** | **Exploring the writer's technique**

a) In the first sentence of this advice text, the writer uses the clause 'please take extra care' (line 2).

   i. What verb form is being used here? -

   ii. Rewrite this phrase to make it sound more urgent and important.

   -

b) In the section about flags, the writer uses the word 'Never' to emphasise instructions. Pick out three imperative verbs that are used with 'never'.

-    -   -

c) Rewrite the advice below without the bullet points and with the imperative phrasal verb at the beginning of each point.

  • **Sunscreen** – slop on SPF 30+ broad-spectrum waterproof sunscreen every 2 hours

  -

  • **Sun hat** – slap on a broad-brimmed hat that shades your face, neck and ears

  -

d) Look at your answers to part c. Do you think the rewritten sentences are more or less effective? Why?

- -

✏ **Activity 3** | **Try it yourself**

On separate paper, write your own short advice text. It could be advice for cyclists, pedestrians or explorers on how to stay safe. In your text, include:

• at least two imperatives (giving instructions)

• at least two phrasal verbs (such as 'look after', 'find out', 'mess about with', 'take care').

5 Participles

What are participles?

Every verb in English has two participles:

- the present participle, which always ends **–ing**, such as **walking, taking, building**

- the past participle, which often ends **–ed** or **–en** or **–t**, such as **walked, taken, built**.

How do they work?

The terms 'present participle' and 'past participle' can be confusing, because they don't necessarily link to the past or present tense. For example:

I am **running**.
> present participle used as part of the **present** progressive form

I was **running**.
> present participle used as part of the **past** progressive form

Find out more

There is more about the progressive forms on page 18.

Past participles can be used in the active or passive voice. For example:

I have **walked** into a tree.
> past participle in the active voice

I was almost **eaten** by a tiger.
> past participle used in the passive voice

Present and past participles can also be used as adjectives. For example:

It is a **boring** job.
> present participle of the verb 'to bore' used as an adjective

The teacher felt **confused**.
> past participle of the verb 'to confuse' used as an adjective

Find out more

There is more about the active and passive on page 22.

Activity 1

Circle the present participle in each sentence below. There may be more than one in some sentences. Remember a participle can also be used as an adjective.

a) The cook is stirring her broth and decides it needs a pinch more of pepper.

b) Yasmin was travelling happily but knew her voyage must end eventually.

c) The unicorn, who hides in the forest by day, is now galloping in the fields.

d) I am sitting quietly at the table to finish my homework. My sister is telling me that I am a teacher's pet. I am not listening.

/6

Activity 2

Complete the following sentences by changing the infinitive form of the verb (which is in brackets) to the past participle. The first example has been done for you.

a) Pooja and Blake's climb had (to take) taken several hours.

b) They had (to stand) _____ in the rain for over two hours.

c) They had (to look) _____ up at the towering fortress and had (to exchange) _____ uneasy glances with each other.

d) Then the door had (to open) _____ and they had (to gasp) _____ in astonishment at the figure before them.

e) It was the strange man who had (to write) _____ the first prophecy.

/6

Activity 3

Write the past and present participles for the verbs below.

	Present participle	Past participle
a) To ride	riding	ridden
b) To see		
c) To throw		
d) To run		
e) To drive		

/8

Tip

Remember that the past participle can differ from the simple past tense form. Check it works with the words 'I had...' before it.

6 The progressive (continuous) forms

What are progressive forms?

The progressive form of verbs shows that something is happening or was happening in an ongoing manner. For example:

present progressive — I **am playing** my cello.

past progressive — I **was playing** my cello.

How do they work?

The progressive form uses two verbs:

- a form of the auxiliary verb 'to be'
- the present participle of a main verb.

For example:

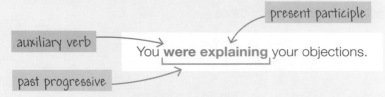

present participle

auxiliary verb

You **were explaining** your objections.

past progressive

Find out more

There is more about participles on page 16.

The form of the auxiliary verb 'to be' changes according to the subject and the tense. For the present progressive form, the auxiliary verb should be **am**, **are** or **is**, e.g. 'she is running', or 'they are running'. For the past progressive form, the auxiliary verb should be **was** or **were**, e.g. 'she was running' or 'they were running'.

The present progressive form is often used for something that is happening or has happened over a long period of time. For example:

Year 9 students **are training** for the county matches.

present progressive

The past progressive form is often used when an action is interrupted by something else. For example:

past progressive

You **were explaining** your objections when a phoenix landed on your shoulder.

✏ Activity 1

Read the statements below and decide whether they are true or false.
Tick the correct answer.

	True	False
a) The present progressive form describes an action that has been completed.		
b) The present progressive form describes an action that is ongoing.		
c) 'I was swimming in the balmy sea' is an example of the past progressive form.		
d) The past progressive form describes an action that was ongoing, such as, 'The mice were planning their attack.'		

/4

✏ Activity 2

Circle the auxiliary verb and underline the present participle in each sentence below. The first one has been done for you.

a) I (am) hoping that she doesn't discover my deceit.

b) They are racing towards the finish line.

c) James was painting the garage door purple.

d) Is she really drawing a picture of me?

/6

Tip

Remember that the auxiliary verb 'to be' is irregular. Its different forms are **am**, **is**, **are**, **was**, **were**.

✏ Activity 3

The sentences below are written in the simple past tense.

- **Circle the subject of the verb and underline the main verb in each sentence.**

- **Rewrite each sentence in the past progressive form by:**

    - **changing the main verb to a present participle**

    - **adding the past form of the auxiliary verb *to be*.**

The first example has been done for you.

a) (Yannis) completed his equations.   Yannis was completing his equations.

b) You read your book quietly. _____

c) Marwa complained bitterly. _____

d) They spoke the truth. _____

e) Katie inspected the engine. _____

/12

7 Subject and verb agreement

What is subject and verb agreement?

The subject is usually the person or thing that is carrying out the action or process of the verb.

subject

verb

The **Prime Minister ignores** the question.

The verb is said 'to agree' with the subject when the form of the verb is correct for the subject of the verb.

How does it work?

The verb form sometimes changes, depending on whether the subject is either singular or plural and in the first, second or third person.

Subject	Singular	Plural
First person	I **sit**	we **sit**
Second person	you **sit**	you **sit**
Third person	he/she/it **sits**	they **sit**

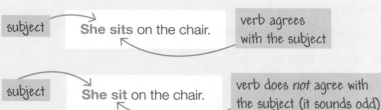

subject

She sits on the chair.

verb agrees with the subject

subject

She sit on the chair.

verb does *not* agree with the subject (it sounds odd)

"The subject should always agree with the verb!"

"I agree!"

SUBJECT   VERB

Tip

To complete some of the sentences in Activities 2 and 3, you will need to use the correct form of the verb 'to be'.
You may find the table below helpful.

Subject	Present	Simple past
I	am	was
you	are	were
she/he/it	is	was
we	are	were
they	are	were

Activity 1

Read the statements below and decide whether they are true or false.
Tick the correct answer.

	True	False
a) When we say 'the verb must agree with the subject', we mean that the correct form of the verb must match with the thing or person doing the verb.		
b) In the sentence, 'Aaron trimmed his fingernails', the fingernails are the subject of the verb.		
c) The sentence 'Sara eat her sandwich' is wrong because the verb does not agree with the subject.		
d) The verb is most likely to change form when the subject is in the third person singular.		

/4

Activity 2

The sentences below lack subject and verb agreement. Circle the verb that is wrong and rewrite the sentence correctly below. The first one has been done for you.

a) Those two windows (is) open.   _Those two windows are open._

b) I were going to apologise to her, honestly.

----

c) Was you listening to me?

----

d) There is scorpions in the desert.

----

e) Vanda think carefully about the choice before her.

----

f) Were he thinking what I were thinking?

/11

Activity 3

Write two sentences including a form of the verb 'to be'. Circle the subject of each sentence and underline the verb or verbs, checking that they agree.

a) ---

----

b) ---

/6

8 Active and passive voices

What are the active and passive voices?

A sentence is in the active voice when the subject is the person or thing doing something. In the active voice, the subject usually comes before the verb. For example:

subject of the verb   verb   object of the verb

Naftali painted a picture.

A sentence is in the passive voice when there is more emphasis on what is done and to whom or what, rather than who does it. For example:

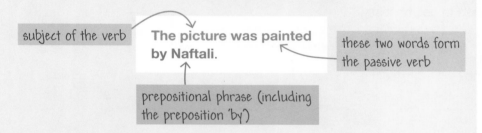

subject of the verb   **The picture was painted by Naftali.**   these two words form the passive verb

prepositional phrase (including the preposition 'by')

Find out more

There is more about subject and verb agreement on page 20. There is more about prepositional phrases on page 34.

Notice that in the passive voice, the subject is the person or thing that would have been the object in the active voice.

How do they work?

We make a verb passive by using the correct form of the auxiliary verb 'to be' or 'to get' plus the past participle of the main verb.

Look at how the verbs change in these two sentences:

Active voice	Passive voice
Shirley **brews** her tea.	The tea **was brewed** by Shirley.
The snow **covered** the footprints.	The footprints **got covered** by the snow.

Notice how the word order has changed. The object of the active verbs, at the end of each sentence, has become the subject of the passive verbs at the start of each sentence. This change in position changes the emphasis.

Activity 1

Read the sentences below and decide whether they are written in the active or passive voice. Tick the correct box. The first one has been done for you.

Sentence	Active voice	Passive voice
a) The minister cleared her throat.	✔	
b) The chocolates were eaten by the gluttons.		
c) The parcel was passed by Charlotte.		
d) The president read the speech.		
e) Ten thousand fans stamped their feet.		

/4

Activity 2

Read the sentences below. Some are written in the active voice, others in the passive voice. Decide what is the subject, verb, object or prepositional phrase in each sentence and label them. The first example has been done for you.

Subject   Verb   Object
↓   ↓   ↓
a) Ozzi   threw   the sandwich.

b) The new swimming pool was opened by the mayor.

c) Raheema piloted the plane.

d) The yeti poured her cereal.

e) The worms were eaten by the birds.

/12

Activity 3

The four sentences below are all written in the active voice. Underline the object of the verb in each sentence. Then, rewrite each sentence in the passive voice. The first example has been done for you.

a) The Hoodlum Harpies play ice hockey every week.

   Ice hockey is played every week by the Hoodlum Harpies.

b) Julie climbs every mountain in Wales. _____

c) Xander ate all the food. _____

d) The professors translate the symbols on the parchment. _____

_____

/6

23

9 Adverbs and adverbials

What are adverbs and adverbials?

An adverb describes a verb, an adjective or another adverb. They often, but not always, end in **–ly**. For example:

| adverb | Tahima **carefully opened** her umbrella. | verb |

| adjective | The changing room was **revoltingly smelly**. | adverb |

| adverbs | Carlos boasted about his achievements **really tactlessly**. |

An adverbial is an adverb, clause or phrase that gives more information about a verb. Adverbials can be made up of more than one word and do not have to include an adverb.

How do they work?

Adverbials typically provide information about when, where, how or why an action is carried out. They can take the form of an adverb or adverb phrase, such as in the example below.

The mountaineer climbed **much too recklessly**.

adverbial – the adverb phrase tells us *how* the mountaineer climbed

Adverbials can also take the form of prepositional phrases, for example:

The mountaineer climbed **up the sheer rock face**.

adverbial – the prepositional phrase tells us *where* the mountaineer climbed

Adverbials can also take the form of noun phrases and subordinate clauses.

The mountaineer climbed **all day**.

adverbial – the noun phrase tells us *when* the mountaineer climbed

The mountaineer climbed **in order to reach the top**.

adverbial – the subordinate clause tells us *why* the mountaineer climbed

Tip

While an adverb can give more information about a verb, an adjective or another adverb, an adverbial can only give more information about a verb.

Find out more

Find out more about prepositional phrases on page 34, noun phrases on page 6 and subordinate clauses on page 38.

Activity 1

Read the sentences listed in the table below. Underline the adverbs in each sentence. Tick whether the adverb is describing a verb, an adjective or another adverb. The first example has been done for you.

Sentence	Describing a verb	Describing an adjective	Describing an adverb
a) Arthur felt <u>completely</u> calm when he succeeded his father as King.		✔	
b) The tyrannosaurus hungrily devoured the scones.			
c) Parvez was terribly envious of his brother's achievements.			
d) The boss completely forgot to mention Donna's contribution to the firm's success.			
e) He very gently moved the injured fox.			
f) Dad absent-mindedly dunked the biscuit in his coffee.			

/10

Activity 2

Underline the adverbial in each of the sentences below.

a) The wind blew very fiercely.

b) They went on holiday yesterday morning.

c) Mo cheered when his team scored.

d) We all slept under the stars.

/4

Activity 3

Add an adverbial to each of the sentences below. For each example, make sure you use the adverbial type mentioned in brackets.

a) Nora grabbed her umbrella _____.
(adverbial to show why)

b) Kaylee will repair the starship _____.
(adverbial to show when)

c) The mouse squeaked _____.
(adverbial to show how)

d) Nish ate his dinner _____.
(adverbial to show where)

/4

Adverbs and adverbials in context

Extract from 'Napoleon and the Spectre' by Charlotte Brontë, 1833

The following extract is taken from the opening of a short story about French Emperor Napoleon, who believes he meets a ghost.

Scarcely had he settled into a peaceful attitude of **repose**, when he was disturbed by a sensation of thirst. Lifting himself on his elbow, he took a glass of lemonade from the small stand which was placed beside him. He refreshed himself by a deep **draught**. As he returned the goblet to its station a deep groan burst from a kind of
5 **closet** in one corner of the apartment.

"Who's there?" cried the Emperor, seizing his pistols. "Speak […]."

This threat produced no other effect than a short, sharp laugh, and a dead silence followed.

The Emperor started from his couch, and, hastily throwing on a **robe-de-chambre**
10 which hung over the back of a chair, stepped courageously to the haunted closet. As he opened the door something rustled. He sprang forward sword in hand. No soul or even substance appeared, and the rustling, it was evident, had proceeded from the falling of a cloak, which had been suspended by a peg from the door.

Half ashamed of himself, he returned to bed.

15 Just as he was about once more to close his eyes, the light of the three wax **tapers**, which burned in a silver branch over the mantlepiece, was suddenly darkened. He looked up. A black, **opaque** shadow obscured it. Sweating with terror, the Emperor put out his hand to seize the **bell-rope**, but some invisible being snatched it rudely from his grasp, and at the same instant the **ominous** shade vanished.

repose rest	**robe-de-chambre** dressing gown	**bell-rope** a bell used to summon servants
draught drink	**tapers** candles	**ominous** threatening
closet cupboard	**opaque** not able to be seen through	

✏ Activity 1 Understanding the text

a) What disturbs the Emperor from his rest?

----

b) How does the Emperor react to the noise he hears?

----

c) What does he decide has made the noise?

----

d) How does he feel when he sees the shadow?

✏ Activity 2   Exploring the writer's technique

a) Identify three adverbs in the text that describe a verb and decide what effect they create
for the reader. Complete the table below. The first example has been done for you.

Adverb	Effect
scarcely	Suggests that the Emperor has hardly had time to fall asleep

b) i. In what state of mind does the Emperor return to bed?

----

   ii. Rewrite this sentence from the extract, moving the adverb phrase to the
end of the sentence.

     Half-ashamed of himself, he returned to bed.

----

  iii. How does changing the position of the adverbial affect the sentence? Think
about what is being emphasised most and where this emphasis is placed.

----

c) Select an adverbial from the text that:

   i. helps us to picture the way in which the Emperor performs an action --------------------------

  ii. conveys a sense of time --

 iii. suggests how the Emperor is feeling --

✏ Activity 3   Try it yourself

On a separate piece of paper, write about a time when something surprising happened to you.

Use a range of adverbs and adverbials to give more detail about actions and events.

10 Adjectives and adjective phrases

What are adjectives and adjective phrases?

Adjectives describe nouns or pronouns. These are all adjectives:

comfortable   luxurious   generous   happy   dangerous

How do they work?

Adjectives usually come before a noun.

a **solid** wall   **fresh** flowers

They can also be used with the verb 'to be' after a pronoun.

He is **peaceful**.

Adjective phrases (also known as adjectival phrases)

An adjective phrase is a phrase that has an adjective as its head or key word. The other words in the phrase can be made up of adverbs and other adjectives.

adjective phrase with 'good' as its head word

Shimon's school report was **quite good** this term.

adjective phrase with 'poor' as its head word

The wombat's handwriting was **very poor**.

adjective phrase with 'green' as its head word

It was an **unbelievably luminous green** creature.

Note that 'quite', 'very' and 'unbelievably' are all adverbs that tell us about the quality of the main adjective.

Tip

Remember, it is important not to overuse a particular technique in your writing. For example, two or three adjective phrases in a row would be too much.

Activity 1

Fill in the gaps below with appropriate adjectives.

The knight gloomily surveyed the _____ landscape. Nothing but a plain of _____ boulders and _____ sand. Where was the _____ oasis that the _____ merchant had assured him was situated here? He sighed, dug his heels into the sides of his _____ horse and prepared to canter across the _____ scene.

/7

Activity 2

Circle the adjective phrase in each of the following sentences.

a) Your suggestion that we should paint the house pink is utterly ridiculous.

b) I am totally inspired by that film.

c) The rumour, which was entirely untruthful, was nevertheless all over the school by lunchtime.

d) The decoration of the birthday cake was absolutely perfect.

e) Nadia was genuinely aghast at the consequences of her behaviour.

f) Mum's enthusiastic use of the hair clippers had left Jean-Luc absolutely bald.

/6

Activity 3

Write a sentence to include each of the adjective phrases below.

a) extremely reluctant

----

b) quite lazy

----

c) very enthusiastic

----

d) completely unnecessary

----

e) rather tired

/5

Adjectives and adjective phrases in context

Extract from *Idle Thoughts of an Idle Fellow* from the essay 'On the Weather' by Jerome K. Jerome, published 1886

Jerome K. Jerome was a famous essayist. Here he considers the topic of the British weather.

It certainly is most wretched weather. [...]

Yet I think it is only to us in cities that all weather is so unwelcome. In her own home, the country, Nature is sweet in all her moods. What can be more beautiful than the snow, falling big with mystery in silent softness, decking the fields and trees with white
5   as if for a fairy wedding! [...] And oh, how dainty is spring—Nature at sweet eighteen!

When the little hopeful leaves peep out so fresh and green, so pure and bright, like young lives pushing shyly out into the bustling world; when the fruit-tree blossoms, pink and white, like village maidens in their Sunday frocks, hide each whitewashed cottage in a cloud of fragile splendour; and the cuckoo's note upon the breeze is
10   wafted through the woods! And summer, with its deep dark green and drowsy hum— when the rain-drops whisper solemn secrets to the listening leaves and the twilight lingers in the lanes! And autumn! Ah, how sadly fair, with its golden glow and the dying grandeur of its tinted woods—its blood-red sunsets and its ghostly evening mists, with its busy murmur of **reapers**, and its **laden** orchards, and the calling of
15   the **gleaners**, and the festivals of praise!

reapers harvesters
laden heavily loaded or weighed down (with fruit)

gleaners workers who pick up grain left behind by the harvesters

---

✏ Activity 1   Understanding the text

a) What does Jerome believe about the weather in the countryside compared to the weather in the city?

------

b) What does he compare the snow-covered countryside to? ------

c) What does he like about autumn?

✏ Activity 2   Exploring the writer's technique

a) This text contains a wide range of adjectives.

    i. Underline six adjectives that you can find.

    ii. Select three adjectives you think are especially good at creating a picture for the reader and explain why each is effective.

----

b) Re-read the following phrases in the source text opposite: 'the little hopeful leaves' (line 6) and 'And autumn! Ah, how sadly fair…' (line 12)

    i. Underline the adjective phrase.

    ii. Circle the head word in each adjective phrase (remember that it must be an adjective).

    iii. One student wrote:

> The first of these adjective phrases 'little hopeful' describes the early promise of spring and helps the reader to build up a detailed picture in their mind.

    How does the second of these phrases help to convey a sense of atmosphere?

----

c) Re-read the adjective phrases 'so fresh and green, so pure and bright' (line 6). How do these phrases help to emphasise the writer's point? Think about the way the writer has structured the adjective phrases and the connotations (associations) of the words.

✏ Activity 3   Try it yourself

On a separate piece of paper, write about your favourite season of the year.

Include adjectives and adjective phrases to emphasise your ideas and add detail to your description.

You might include adjective phrases such as the ones below.

the most stunning   absolutely beautiful   warm, balmy and relaxing   icy, freezing

11 Determiners

What are determiners?

A determiner comes before a noun and gives us more information about it, such as: which one it is, how many there are, where it is and whose it is.

the	a	an	my	your	enough	more
less	each	any	some	that	whose	

Tip

The determiners **a**, **an** and **the** are also called articles.

How do they work?

Possessive determiners

Possessive determiners tell us about ownership.

my	your	his	her	its	our	their

My castle is crumbling.

Quantifying determiners

Quantifying determiners tell us about the quantity or number.

enough	fewer	less	forty-two

There are **enough** players for the team.

Looking at the mountain, **her** brother soon realised that **this** trek was going to take a long time.

Demonstrative determiners

Demonstrative determiners show us (demonstrate) which one by saying whether it is near or far.

this	these	that	those
this game	**these** wolves	**that** sofa	**those** clowns

Note that **this**, **that**, **those**, **these** can be used as demonstrative determiners *and* demonstrative pronouns. It is easy to confuse the two. However, a demonstrative determiner always comes before a noun or a noun phrase.

Look at **that** mountain. → demonstrative determiner

A demonstrative pronoun stands alone in place of a noun.

Look at **that**. → demonstrative pronoun

Find out more

There is more about demonstrative pronouns on page 10.

Activity 1

Circle the determiner in each of the following sentences. Then decide what type of determiner it is and tick the appropriate box. The first example has been completed.

Sentence	Possessive determiner	Quantifying determiner	Demonstrative determiner
a) (Three) dogs sat forlornly outside.		✔	
b) Go and collect those children from school.			
c) I will decorate my hat with ivy.			
d) It's time to move that toybox upstairs.			
e) Many fans turned up to watch.			
f) When are you going to write your novel?			

/10

Activity 2

Fill in each of the blanks in this paragraph with one of the quantifying determiners below. Cross out each one as you use it.

enough   some   fewer   less   three   many

Although many students had already had _____ to eat (some of them had had no

_____ than _____ helpings each), _____ of them still wanted more. However,

_____ of them asked for _____ chocolate sauce this time, saying a pint was too much.

/6

Activity 3

'This', 'that', 'those' and 'these' can be used as demonstrative determiners or as demonstrative pronouns. One of these words is in italics in each sentence that follows. Tick the correct description of the word after each sentence.

Sentence	Determiner	Pronoun
a) Can you see *this*?		
b) Can you see *this* fish?		
c) Who is *that* comedian?		
d) *That* is my phone.		
e) Where are *those* alligators?		
f) What are *these* ugly creatures?		
g) What are *these*?		

/7

12 Prepositions and prepositional phrases

What are prepositions and prepositional phrases?

A preposition comes before a noun, a pronoun or a noun phrase and links it to other words in the sentence.

How do they work?

Prepositions can tell us about the position or direction of something, such as:

on	outside	alongside	between	through

Prepositions can tell us about timing, such as:

since	while	during	at	following

Prepositions can show a link or relationship between things, and can be a phrase:

against	by	with	concerning	in spite of	according to

Prepositional phrases

A prepositional phrase is a group of words that has a preposition as its head word.

preposition

The mouse ran **up** the clock.

prepositional phrase

preposition

prepositional phrase

The robots have no real enemies, **except for** scrap metal merchants.

preposition

In spite of your interference, we will still triumph.

prepositional phrase

Activity 1

**Add prepositions in the appropriate places in the paragraph below.
The prepositions needed are listed below.**

| throughout | by | since | at | until |

They hadn't had tea _____ yesterday and there had been tea without biscuits _____ the

winter. But _____ four o'clock that day, the minions chatted in the café _____ it was time

to resume their patrol. _____ five past five, the café was empty.

/5

Activity 2

**Add prepositions to the paragraph below to show a link or relationship between
things. The prepositions needed are listed below. Note that some can be used
more than once.**

| without | unlike | with | concerning | in spite of | except for |

_____ his minions, the Evil Genius had not had his tea and had drunk nothing _____

stale water all day. He ordered the minions into his throne room. Quite _____ guards, most

of them were trembling. " _____ this matter of tea," grumbled the Evil Genius, "why didn't

you bring me any?" _____ her fear, one of them spoke up.

"We couldn't remember whether you have it _____ or _____ sugar."

/7

Activity 3

a) Underline the four prepositional phrases in the following paragraph of the story.

b) Circle the head word of each prepositional phrase.

Silence fell after her words. Then, incredibly, she spoke again: "And, we were without your
reusable cup. And, according to the Environment Agency, it's bad to use takeaway cups."

The Evil Genius sighed.

"But," the minion continued, "you can have the biscuits minus the tea." She put three custard
creams on the plate and the Evil Genius cheered up.

/8

Prepositions and prepositional phrases in context

Extract from *Attention All Shipping* by Charlie Connelly, published 2004

In this extract, the writer, who is touring all the places mentioned in the shipping forecast, describes the scene from a pub in south-east London.

The **Cutty Sark** pub is a good half mile from the ship that gave it its name, but that doesn't seem to matter. Inside it is dark and timbered, **snugs** here and barrel stools there. A grand wooden staircase sweeps up through the centre, and I like to sit and look out at the river from the huge first floor bay window. Here, it's easy to be
5 lulled into **Greenwich** time, where the days pass more slowly than anywhere else in London. It's late afternoon and the pub is all but empty. The weak, wintry sun is still leaking from behind the Observatory and occasionally will be caught by the brown sails of an old Thames sailing barge making its way along the river. Hundreds of these used to buzz around the coast carrying cargoes of all descriptions right up to
10 the middle of the twentieth century. There are no working barges now but a handful are maintained by a dedicated band of enthusiasts, some still making their dignified way up the Thames for the benefit of tourists, their dark hulls and brown sails almost lost beneath the huge glimmering skyscrapers of Docklands beyond.

If you sit to the left of the window you can see the Millennium Dome looming large on
15 the Greenwich peninsula, and the Thames barge soon disappears behind it. You have to crane your neck a little, but off to the far right you can just make out the two slim, black-tipped silver chimneys of the Tate & Lyle sugar refinery in Silvertown.

Cutty Sark – a 19th-century sailing ship, now a museum ship in south-east London

snugs – cosy seating areas
Greenwich – an area of south-east London

✏ Activity 1   Understanding the text

a) What does the writer like to do when he visits the Cutty Sark pub?

----

b) List three things that the writer sees from the window.

----

c) What time of day is it in this extract?

----

d) What are the Thames barges used for now?

✎ Activity 2   Exploring the writer's technique

a) Re-read from 'The Cutty Sark pub is a good half mile...' (line 1) to '... look out at the river from the huge first floor bay window' (line 4) in the extract opposite.

    i.   Underline three prepositional phrases in this part of the text.

    ii.   How do these phrases help to convey what the pub is like? Tick the statement below that best describes the effect of these phrases.

| ☐ They add detail about the pub and why the writer likes it there. | ☐ They provide instructions on how to get to the pub. | ☐ They explain how to get upstairs. |

b) The writer says he likes to 'look out at the river'. He could have written 'look at the river'. What does the word 'out' add to this phrase?

----

c) In the first paragraph, the writer uses the prepositional phrases 'along the river' and 'around the coast' to describe the movement of the Thames barges. Most barges travel on canals. What do these phrases convey about the flexibility of these barges?

----

d) The writer says, 'their dark hulls and brown sails almost lost beneath the huge glimmering skyscrapers of Docklands beyond' (lines 12–13). What kind of image does the prepositional phrase in this clause create for the reader?

----

e) Using the prepositional phrases 'to the left of the window' and 'off to the far right' to help you, draw a sketch of the writer's position and what he sees. Use a separate piece of paper for this sketch.

✎ Activity 3   Try it yourself

Using some of the prepositional phrases from the extract on page 36 as models, write a description of the view from one of your windows at home. Explain where you are sitting and what you can see. Write your description on a separate piece of paper.

13 Clauses

What are clauses?

A clause is a group of words that work together as a unit with a verb as its head word (key word).

verb as head word → She **grumbled** interminably. ← main clause

How do they work?

A main clause is a clause that contains a subject and a verb, and makes sense on its own. A main clause can form a single-clause sentence or it can be part of a multi-clause sentence.

Ian read it carefully.

A subordinate clause adds information to a main clause but can't work as a sentence on its own:

although he couldn't understand it

However, if we add this subordinate clause to a main clause it makes a complete sentence:

Ian read it carefully although he couldn't understand it.

A subordinate clause starts with a subordinating conjunction, such as:

because	although	though	while	for	before	so
whether	since	after	until	if	as	

Relative clauses

A relative clause is a type of subordinate clause. It starts with one of the following relative pronouns:

which	who	whom	whose	that

relative pronoun → It reminded her of the sports car **that** she used to love so much. ← relative clause

Tip

Remember that every clause contains a verb.

Find out more

There is more about pronouns on page 10.

Relative clauses are sometimes separated off from the rest of the sentence (the main clause) using two commas:

main clause → The dragon, who was very tired by now, crossly blew smoke from its nose. ← relative clause

✏ Activity 1

Underline the relative clauses in each of the sentences below.
Then circle the relative pronoun in each sentence.

a) Tegan, who was naturally very considerate, always gave up her seat for a less able passenger.

b) The jacket that he wore yesterday was Chang Lee's favourite.

c) The sun, which had risen early that morning, was dazzlingly beautiful.

d) The boys, whose faces wore grins of mischief, strolled across the school playing field.

e) The witness, who was very helpful in the case, gave a full statement.

/10

✏ Activity 2

All of the sentences below are multi-clause sentences and contain a subordinate clause. Underline the main clause in each sentence and then identify which sentences contain relative clauses. The first one has been done for you.

Sentence	Contains a relative clause
a) The weather that we had this summer was uncomfortable, but also enjoyable.	✔
b) Whether you like it or not, we are going to see Grandpa this weekend as he is unwell.	
c) Although I'd had a pudding, the peaches, which you bought earlier, were delicious.	
d) I feel inspired to write a poem because the sky is blue.	

/4

✏ Activity 3

Complete the following sentences by adding a relative clause in the space provided.

a) The teacher, whose --, put the whole lot of them in detention.

b) The girl, who --, was taken to hospital.

c) The computer that -- isn't working properly.

/3

14 Single-clause sentences

What are single-clause sentences?

A sentence is a group of words that expresses a complete idea. Sentences can have just one main clause. These are called single-clause sentences or simple sentences.

> It was all a dream.

How do they work?

Single clause-sentences must contain a subject (the noun or pronoun that is doing the action) and a verb.

Some single-clause sentences are very short, but others can be much longer and can include various additional phrases, such as prepositional phrases, noun phrases and adverbials.

The examples below are all single-clause sentences, with just one main verb.

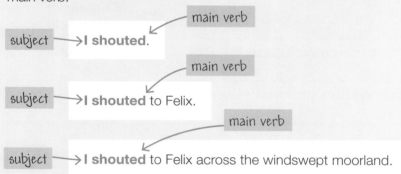

subject → **I shouted**. — main verb

subject → **I shouted** to Felix. — main verb

subject → **I shouted** to Felix across the windswept moorland. — main verb

> Despite my promise, **I shouted** to Felix across the windswept moorland.
>
> subject   main verb

Some writers use short single-clause sentences to give emphasis to a single idea or action. A series of short, single-clause sentences can be used in a story to track a series of events in quick succession. This can help to create a sense of drama or add tension.

> She stared in horror. A wall of water was roaring up the street. She ran.

Tip

Remember that sentences should begin with a capital letter and end with: a full stop to make a statement, a question mark to ask a question or an exclamation mark to express an exclamation.

Tip

The subject is often the noun, noun phrase or pronoun that comes before the verb.

The team won the match.

Activity 1

For each of the single-clause sentences below, underline the verb and circle the subject.

a) Sarah stared at the grey elephant.

b) A pachyderm is a large, thick-skinned mammal.

c) The small cat prowled the streets after midnight.

d) Zulfi and Sadie bought a new telescope from the travelling salesman.

e) In the dead of night, Joseph crept silently towards the door.

f) We are all in this together.

/12

Activity 2

Circle the four single-clause sentences below. Remember that single-clause sentences can be long as well as short.

Please help me.   Against all the odds, he survived for more than a year on Mars, alone.

Zoe rowed the boat while Reggie navigated.

No one believed her.   Lightning tore across the sky and the wind whisked up the sea.

The mysterious woman moved silently towards the woods.

The screen went blank but the voices continued.

/4

Activity 3

Write three separate single-clause sentences. The first should be very short, the second longer and the third as long as you can make it. Remember, each one should contain just one verb.

a) --

b) --

----

c) --

/3

(15) Multi-clause sentences

What are multi-clause sentences?

Multi-clause sentences have more than one clause, each with their own verb. The clauses can be joined by conjunctions or by punctuation such as a semi-colon or colon.

How do they work?

Some multi-clause sentences contain two or more main clauses of equal weight. They are sometimes known as compound sentences. The clauses are joined by coordinating conjunctions such as:

and	but	yet	nor	or

coordinating conjunction

first main clause

second main clause

Dad jumped on the trampoline,
and Lucy crashed into the greenhouse.

Other multi-clause sentences contain one main clause and one or more subordinate clauses. They are sometimes known as complex sentences. Subordinate clauses begin with subordinating conjunctions such as:

after	as	because	so	until
though	since	before	if	

subordinating conjunction

main clause

subordinate clause

We are going to conquer Mars,
after we have finished the crossword.

Find out more

There is more about clauses on page 38.

Find out more

There is more about colons and semi-colons on page 56.

The spaceship was ready for the trip, although the passengers still had to board.

Activity 1

How many clauses are there in each of the sentences below?
Write the correct number of clauses in the box. The first answer
has been completed for you.

a) Lava is hotter than boiling water. `1`

b) As you are very young, I shall overlook your rudeness. ☐

c) Scott and Omar played snooker. ☐

d) The journey, which had begun pleasantly enough,
deteriorated into arguments and tears. ☐

e) Matt, who was cautious with his money, offered to buy
me an ice cream, although I never thought he would. ☐

/4

Tip

Remember that
each clause has
its own verb, so
you might find it
helpful to circle all
the verbs in each
sentence first.

Activity 2

For each of the sentences below, underline all of the main clauses and
circle the subordinate clauses. There may be more than one main clause
in a sentence and sometimes no subordinate clause.

a) We ran quickly but we were too slow to catch the train.

b) Jodie threw away her socks because they were faded and old.

c) Eat all of your vegetables before you leave the table.

d) Amir is running the marathon in April so he trains every morning.

e) It was a cold, crisp morning and the sky was heavy with snow.

f) If you finish your homework, Mum will take you to the cinema but you have to be quick.

/13

Activity 3

Complete these multi-clause sentences by adding another clause.
Then write your own multi-clause sentence.

a) Dad will give us a lift to the shopping centre although _____

b) The bus thundered down the one way street until _____

c) The teacher sprinted to the finish line and _____

d) After plotting our escape _____

e) _____

_____

/6

Sentences in context

Extract from 'When She Is Old and I Am Famous' by Julie Orringer, published 2003

The following extract is the opening of a short story. Here, the narrator describes her younger cousin.

There are grape leaves, like a crown, on her head. Grapes hang in her hair, and in her hands she holds the green vines. She dances with both arms in the air. On her smallest toe she wears a ring of pink shell.

Can someone tell her, please, to go home? This is my Italy and my story. We are in a
5   vineyard near Florence. I have just turned twenty. She is a girl, a gangly teen, and she is a model. She is famous for almost getting killed. Last year, when she was fifteen, a photographer asked her to dance on the rail of a bridge and she fell. A metal rod beneath the water pierced her chest. Water came into the wound, close to her heart, and for three weeks she was in the hospital with an infection so furious it made her
10   chant nonsense. All the while she got thinner and more pale, until, when she emerged, they thought she might be the best model there ever was. Her hair is wavy and long and **buckeye**-brown, and her blue eyes have a stunned, sad look to them. She is five feet eleven inches tall and weighs one hundred and thirteen pounds. She has told me so.

buckeye a type of chestnut tree

✏ Activity 1   Understanding the text

a) Where is this text set?

----

b) What does the narrator's cousin look like?

----

c) How was the narrator's cousin injured?

----

d) Why did some people believe she might be 'the best model there ever was' and why might some people disagree with this opinion?

✏ Activity 2 | Exploring the writer's technique

a) Re-read the final single-clause sentence: 'She has told me so.' (line 13).
What is the effect of this simple sentence? Rank the effects below from 1 to 3, where 1 is the most effective.

| It draws our attention to the cousin's personality. | It conveys the narrator's feelings about her cousin very clearly. | It rounds the paragraph off neatly. |

b) Why does the writer open the second paragraph with a question? Think about:

- the effect on the reader
- what it reveals about the narrator.

----

c) Re-read the part of the text from 'Water came into…' (line 8) to '…the best model there ever was' (line 11).

i. Underline one main clause in these sentences.

ii. Underline one subordinate clause in these sentences.

iii. What is the effect of using longer sentences at this point in the text?

✏ Activity 3 | Try it yourself

On a separate piece of paper, write a short description of someone you know well.
Use a range a sentence types to create variety and interest for your reader.

16 Common mistakes in grammar

I or me?

The pronoun 'I' is used as the subject of a verb:

I devoured the cake. — subject

The pronoun 'me' is used as the object of a verb:

Mum hugged **me**. — object

This rule holds true when there are two or more people as the subject or object:

Jenny and **I** devoured the cake.
Mum hugged **me** and **Sam**.

Those or them?

'Those' is a determiner and is used with plural nouns:

Pass me **those** slippers. — determiner

'Them' is a personal pronoun and is used as the object of the verb:

I like **them**. — pronoun

Is or are?

The verb 'is' should be used with a singular subject (where there is just one).

The window **is** closed. — singular subject

The verb 'are' should be used with a plural subject (where there is more than one).

The windows **are** closed. — plural subject

I can't remember if I'm I or **me**...

Tip

To check whether the pronoun is correct when there are two subjects, cross out one subject to see if the remaining pronoun makes sense on its own. If not, it's the wrong pronoun.

~~Jenny and~~ me devoured the cake. ✗
~~Jenny and~~ I devoured the cake. ✔

✎ Activity 1

Circle the correct pronoun in the sentences below. The first one has been done for you.

a) She passed the puppy to I / (me).

b) I / me am happy to go with you.

c) Make sure you buy the season tickets for Bradley and I / me.

d) Save a piece of cake for Grandpa and I / me.

e) Olenka and I / me explored the space station.

/4

✎ Activity 2

Look at the sentences below. Decide whether they are grammatically correct or incorrect and tick the appropriate description. On separate paper, correct the errors in the incorrect sentences. The first one has been done for you.

	Correct	Incorrect
a) I wish those students would stop talking.	✔	
b) They make more noise than them crows outside.		
c) I gave them more food.		
d) I'm talking about them students.		
e) Pass me those herbal tea bags.		
f) Them ones next to the coffee cups.		

/5

✎ Activity 3

There are one or two grammatical errors in each of the speech bubbles below. Circle the errors and write the correct words above. The first one has been done for you.

are
a) There (is) cows on the road again.

b) Gervais and me will herd them cows back into their field.

c) Yes, I'll make sure them gates is closed properly.

d) He are really fed up.

e) You promised Gervais and I that we could have a break.

/6

1 Capital letters

What are capital letters?

Capital letters are larger, upper-case letters which look **LIKE THIS**. Other letters are smaller, lower-case letters, **like this**.

How do they work?

Capital letters are used for many different reasons.

- For the first letter in a sentence:

  No one wanted to get up that morning.

- For the first person pronoun 'I':

  When can **I** have my breakfast?

- For all proper nouns, such as particular days, months and celebrations:

  Wednesday   **F**ebruary   **N**ew **Y**ear's **D**ay   **E**aster   **E**id al-**F**itr

- For names and titles:

  Freddie   **L**ady **W**orple   **C**onstable **O**ates   **M**s **A**twood

- For key words in the titles of books, films, plays, newspapers, magazines, poems, songs, paintings, sculptures, computer games, such as:

  Charlie and the **C**hocolate **F**actory   **T**he **T**imes
  The **S**tatue of **L**iberty   **M**ona **L**isa

- For brand names, such as retailers and products:

  Rolex   **T**wix   **T**esco   **N**etflix   **A**pple

- For abbreviations and acronyms:

  BBC (British Broadcasting Corporation)   **ITV** (Independent Television)
  NATO (North Atlantic Treaty Organisation)

Let's celebrate **N**ew **Y**ear's **D**ay!

Tip

Common nouns such as dad, mum, grandpa, are all lower case, unless they are used as a name, in which case they take an initial capital.

"My **d**ad is the astronaut," boasted George, before shouting, "Have you initiated the launch sequence, **D**ad?"

✏ Activity 1

The extract below is missing its capital letters. Put them into the correct places. The first one has been done for you.

M

marsha realised constable curlew was following her even before she reached marylebone station. it was christmas eve and the streets were heaving with shoppers. she quickened her pace passing primark, but she couldn't shake off curlew. she ducked into whittaker's newsagents and pretended to browse the magazines: *woodworkers' digest* and *new statesman.* ms whittaker's radio, tuned to the bbc, was playing *have yourself a merry little christmas*. the doorbell rang and marsha whirled round.

/28

✏ Activity 2

In the 18th century, printers tended to capitalise the first letter of all nouns. An 18th-century book containing Shakespeare's plays would have included the extract below from *Julius Caesar*. Circle all the nouns that you would expect to have a lower case letter in a modern version of the play. The first one has been done for you.

Hence, Home, you idle Creatures, get you Home.

Is this a Holiday? What, knew you not

(Being **Mechanical**) you should not walk

Upon a labouring Day without some Sign

Of your Profession?

Hence go away   **Mechanical** labourer

/7

✏ Activity 3

On separate paper, make a check-list to remind yourself of when you should use capital letters.

/7

Tip

The start of each line of text in a Shakespeare play starts with a capital letter, whatever word class it is.

2 Full stops and commas

What are full stops and commas?

A full stop marks the end of a sentence, such as this one.

It can also indicate an abbreviation (shortening) of a word, such as:

> Prof. (Professor)

A comma can be used to:

- separate items in a list
- separate direct speech from information about a speaker
- separate adverbials and clauses within a sentence.

How do they work?

A full stop (or question mark or exclamation mark) should always be used at the end of a sentence.

Commas are often used to separate adverbials and clauses within sentences.

comma after an adverbial → To her dismay, she had forgotten her purse.

While she was sleeping, the bears stole her picnic. ← comma after a subordinate clause

commas to mark the start and finish of the embedded subordinate clause → Giovanni, who could always spot a shoplifter, kept his eyes on the shifty-looking customer.

Comma splicing

Commas should not be used to separate two or more main clauses. This is an error known as comma splicing. For example:

main clause 1 → **Roseanna finished her homework, she then went up to her bedroom. ✗** ← main clause 2

To separate main clauses, use a full stop, semi-colon or other end punctuation, such as an exclamation mark.

Roseanna finished her homework. ← full stop
She then went up to her bedroom. ✔

Find out more

There is more about direct speech on page 60.

Find out more

There is more about adverbials on page 24 and clauses on page 38.

Activity 1

Decide whether the following statements about full stops and commas are true or false and tick the correct box.

	True	False
a) Full stops can be used to separate a subordinate clause from a main clause in a sentence.		
b) Commas can be used to separate items in a list.		
c) Full stops can be used to mark the end of a sentence.		
d) Commas should be used to separate two main clauses.		
e) A pair of commas should be used at the start and end of an embedded subordinate clause.		

/5

Activity 2

Add commas in the correct places to the sentences below. Some sentences might require two commas. The first one has been done for you.

a) Overnight, the rain had transformed the campsite into a field of mud.

b) The ogre who was very watchful regarded the travellers thoughtfully.

c) Fortunately I was able to withstand her sarcasm.

d) When Ellie's foot slid off the cliff edge we all thought she was doomed.

e) Yasmin's design once everyone had thought about it was voted the best.

/6

Activity 3

Correct the punctuation in the essay below, which contains some comma splicing.

In Shakespeare's play 'The Merchant of Venice' we are introduced to the character Bassanio, Bassanio is a young man who is in love with Portia, the trouble is that Bassanio himself doesn't have enough money to impress Portia, who is very wealthy, Bassanio therefore asks his friend Antonio for a loan, but the sum is so high – three thousand ducats – that Antonio cannot help him, Antonio suggests that they ask Shylock for a loan, Shylock is happy to help but says that if Antonio can't pay the money back the forfeit will be one pound (half a kilo) of his flesh.

Tip

Think about capital letters as well as full stops and commas.

Be careful! Not all the commas in this extract are used incorrectly.

/4

3 Parenthesis

What is parenthesis?

A parenthesis adds separate information to a sentence.

You can show a parenthesis in three ways:

- with two round brackets (like this) around the extra information
- with two commas, like this, around the extra information
- with two dashes – like this – around the extra information.

The word or words inside the brackets, commas or dashes can be said to be 'in parenthesis'.

Tip

The plural of parenthesis is parentheses.

How does it work?

You can use parentheses to add information, a comment, a reference, a date or an afterthought. For example:

Apollo 8 – **the second manned space mission** – was the first spacecraft to orbit the moon.

> parenthesis explains what Apollo 8 is

The poem 'Ode to an Expiring Frog' **(on page 72)** is the worst in the whole collection.

> parenthesis adds a page reference

A complete sentence can also be in parenthesis. If you take out the words that are in parenthesis, the sentence should still make sense. Note that its final punctuation needs to go inside the second bracket.

Doctor Who was first screened in 1963 and is the longest-running science-fiction programme in the world. (***Star Trek** ran for three seasons from 1966–69; **Doctor Who** has reached a total of 37 seasons.*)

> parenthesis gives more detailed information

If you take out the words that are in parenthesis, the sentence should still make sense.

The King was given various expensive items (e.g. a crown) to wear on a daily basis.

Activity 1

Decide whether the statements below about parentheses are true or false.
Tick your answer.

	True	False
a) Parentheses are always marked by brackets.		
b) Brackets, dashes and commas can all be used to mark parentheses.		
c) A parenthesis adds extra information to a sentence.		
d) The plural of parenthesis is parentheses.		
e) A parenthesis is always at the end of a sentence.		

/5

Activity 2

Rewrite the sentences in Column A to include the information in Column B
in parenthesis. Use a variety of punctuation to include the parentheses.
The first example has been completed for you.

Column A: Sentences	Column B: Parenthesis
Charles Dickens campaigned to improve the lot of the poor.	1812–1870
Cressida was escorted out of the school.	whose blue hair was forbidden but striking
Take the A142 to Banbury.	the road which is first right after the church
The rabbits decided to go to London.	eager for an adventure
Mr Oswald ordered the students out of the classroom.	despite his promise
Please turn to Act 2 Scene 3 of the play.	page 76

a) <u>Charles Dickens (1812–1870) campaigned to improve the lot of the poor.</u>

b) --

c) --

d) --

e) --

f) --

/5

Activity 3

On a separate piece of paper, write three sentences, each of which should
include parenthesis. The first sentence should be about your home; the
second sentence about your interests; the third sentence can be about
anything you like.

/3

Parenthesis in context

Extract from 'Let's put the brakes on teen drivers and make them wait until they are older' by Joanna Moorhead, *The Guardian*, 11 October 2013

The following text is from an article that argues against lowering the age at which teenagers can learn to drive.

But now, at last, sanity is starting to **prevail**. A government report, by the Transport Research Laboratory, has recommended raising the age at which kids can learn to drive to 18. My 15-year-old daughter, who is counting the months until she's almost 17 (the application can go in three months before their birthday) will be devastated
5   when she hears the news – and so will thousands of other teens, for whom getting a licence and learning to drive is seen as a rite of passage.

But I use the word 'kids' deliberately. Anyone who has older children – and I have two, aged 21 and 19 – knows they are really toddlers in an extraordinarily effective disguise. They look (especially if you don't currently have one) so adult! All grown-
10   up! But – and there's an increasing amount of research to back this up – until they're at least 21, their brains are still in formation. They don't yet "think" like adults; in particular, they don't connect "actions" and "consequences". If you're a driver, you know how bad that could be.

prevail – to be more powerful or frequent

✏ Activity 1   Understanding the text

a) What has a government report recommended?

----

b) How old are the writer's three children?

----

c) When can a teenager apply for a licence to learn to drive?

----

d) At what age does research indicate that a brain is fully formed?

✏ **Activity 2   Exploring the writer's technique**

a) Re-read the first sentence of the text. Why are the words 'at last' placed between commas?

----

b) In the second sentence, the writer again uses parenthesis. Identify the information in parenthesis and explain why the writer has used parenthesis here.

----

c) The writer adds the information '– and I have two, aged 21 and 19 –' in the second paragraph. What effect does this additional information have on the reader?

----

d) Match the following quotations from the text with the reason for placing the words in parenthesis:

'(the application can go in three months before their birthday)'	adds information
'(especially if you don't currently have one)'	supports her argument
'– and there's an increasing amount of research to back this up –'	provides an afterthought

✏ **Activity 3   Try it yourself**

On a separate piece of paper, write an email to your MP explaining why you think the driving age should be raised. Include some of the following extra information, using different forms of parenthesis:

- teen drivers aged 16 to 19 are nearly three times more likely to crash
- teenage brains are still developing
- cars are expensive to run
- 17-year-olds are still in education and don't need a car
- young drivers are more likely to drive at night.

You could also include information from the article on page 54.

4 Colons and semi-colons

What are colons and semi-colons?

A colon looks like this **:**

A semi-colon looks like this **;**

When reading aloud, the colon and semi-colon both show a pause.

How do they work?

Colon

A colon can be used to introduce things, such as a list, a speech, a quotation, an example or an explanation.

> Don't come back without the shopping: bread, cheese and fruit.

colon introduces a list

> Tazeem said: "I have come back to tell you everything."

colon introduces speech

> There are no more trains to Llanfairfach: the branch line was closed in 1962.

colon introduces an explanation

Semi-colon

A semi-colon links together two main clauses that are closely related. It shows a stronger relationship between the clauses than a full stop.

> That car's thirty years old; it's bound to break down.

semi-colon shows a relationship between the age of the car and its likelihood of breaking down

A semi-colon can also be used to separate detailed items in a list. For example:

> The Principal listed his objections: the students' insolence; the staff's laziness; the absence of his favourite cereal at breakfast time.

Tip

Remember that there is no need for a capital letter after a colon or semi-colon unless the next word is a proper noun.

Activity 1

Each of the sentences in the table below contains a colon. Tick what the colon introduces in each sentence.

Sentence	Direct speech	Quotation	List	Explanation
a) There are many legends of lost worlds and cities: Atlantis, El Dorado, Gallifrey.			✔	
b) She snapped: "What's it got to do with you?"	✔			
c) Tricky Trains Limited is sorry that no trains will be running tomorrow: it's too much trouble to provide a good service.				✔
d) This is the beginning of a famous speech by Hamlet: "To be or not to be, that is the question."		✔		
e) She got the best part in the play: her singing was incredible.				✔

5 /5

Activity 2

The following sentences need a colon or a semi-colon. Add the correct punctuation mark in the spaces below.

a) We need to buy all of this at the agricultural fair **:** a tractor, a combine harvester, three shire horses and an apple press.

b) Dad looked at the malfunctioning monitor in despair **;** his daughter would have to fix it.

c) The grey dawn crept gloomily over the garden **:** it was snowing again.

d) Keats wrote **:** 'Beauty is truth, truth beauty'.

4 /4

Activity 3

Write two sentences about what you have done today. The first sentence should include a colon; the second sentence should include a semi-colon.

a) Today we got lots of homework at school: Russian, English, Music and Geography

b) My dad could not drive me to school today; I had to take the bus.

2 /2

5 Apostrophes

What are apostrophes?

Apostrophes are punctuation marks that can show:

- contraction (that words have been shortened)
- possession (that something belongs to someone or something else).

How do they work?

Apostrophes for contraction show where letters have been taken out of words when they are combined and shortened. For example:

is not becomes **isn't**

apostrophe in place of the missing letter 'o'

Some other commonly contracted words are:

have	→	've	**I've** had enough cake.
is	→	's	**She's** very cross.
will	→	'll	**They'll** want salt and vinegar crisps.
are	→	're	**You're** just like my mother.

Apostrophes for possession show ownership. For example:

The **explorer's** chocolate

apostrophe goes after the possessing noun (the explorer), and before the 's'

When the possessing noun is a plural, the apostrophe goes after the final letter, which is often, but not always, 's'.

All of the **teachers'** enthusiasm

If the plural noun does not end in an **–s** or **–es**, the apostrophe still goes after the final letter of the word and before a final 's'.

The **children's** toys

Tip

Apostrophes are never used to make plurals!

This is a very common mistake:

Fresh apple's 90p a kilo ✗

Fresh apples 90p a kilo ✔

ORANGES 95p A KILO

ORANGES 95p A KILO

Mr Smith's oranges cost only 95p a kilo.

Activity 1

Make three contractions from the words below and use them in three different sentences.

| will not | he will | she would | they are | you have |

1) To enter the theatre you've got to have a ticket. ✓

2) He'll behave like a fool just like he always does. ✓

3) I won't let her have her way because she doesn't deserve it. ✓

3/3

Activity 2

Add an apostrophe to show possession in each phrase below.

a) Margaret's crown ✓

b) That fortress's iron gate ✓

c) Both horses' saddles ✓

d) The peoples' choice ✗

e) That lioness's amber eyes ✓

4/5

Activity 3

a) In the sentences below, tick the apostrophes that are used correctly and cross those that are used incorrectly. The first one has been done for you.

     ✗   ✓   ✓

i. I dont and I can't and I won't.

  ✗✓   ✗✓

ii. We're you planning on eating those banana's?

  ✗✓   ✓✓

iii. Hasnt he finished copying Michael's homework?

    ✓✗   ✓✓

iv. The childrens' coats were all over the floor. Only the teacher's was hung up on a peg.

b) Choose one of your crossed contractions and explain why it is incorrect.

Banana's is incorrect because ~~the writer wants to~~ you don't need an apostrophe if it is a plural. ✓

6/7

6 Direct speech and reported speech

What are direct speech and reported speech?

Direct speech uses inverted commas (speech marks) to mark the exact words that someone says.

Reported speech (or indirect speech) reports what has been said, without inverted commas and not necessarily using the exact words spoken.

How do they work?

Direct speech can be introduced by a comma or colon. The inverted commas enclose the exact words that someone says and the final punctuation appears within the inverted commas. For example:

> The squire said, "Put on your armour, get on your horse and ride to defend your queen."

If this were reported speech, it might be written like this:

note how this replaces the word 'said'

> The squire **told her to** put on **her** armour, get on **her** horse and ride to defend **her** queen.

note how the pronoun changes from 'your'

In reported speech, the word 'that' often introduces what was said.

> The President said **that** he would make a firm decision that day.

Questions that are reported lose their question marks. They become statements.

> The President asked his wife: "Will you pass me the chocolate buttons, please**?**"

question mark in direct speech

> The President asked his wife if she would please pass him the chocolate buttons.

full stop indicates the end of the statement

Activity 1

Reported speech is often used by journalists and newspapers to summarise what has been said. For example:

The Leader of the Opposition, Mr Saxon, said that the Prime Minister had no idea how to get the country out of this mess. Replying, the Prime Minister said that Mr Saxon had no evidence of this.

Write the exact words that were said in the speech bubbles below.

Mr Saxon

Prime Minister

/2

Activity 2

Each of the sentences below contains direct speech. Rewrite each sentence into reported speech. The first example has been done for you.

a) "I'm so tired," he announced. "I'm going to have to take a nap."

He announced that he was so tired he would have to take a nap.

b) "Sir," protested the students, "you can't take a nap now!"

----

c) "Oh, fine then. Get out your textbooks and plug in your brains," he replied.

/2

Activity 3

Change the following sentences from reported speech to direct speech. Punctuate your new sentences carefully. The first one has been done for you.

a) Amanda asked Ibrahim if he had seen episode four of *Homeworld*.

"Have you seen episode four of *Homeworld*?" Amanda asked Ibrahim.

b) Ibrahim said that he didn't want her to tell him the plot as he hadn't watched it yet.

----

c) Amanda told him enthusiastically that it was really good.

----

d) Ibrahim said he would try to catch up with it at the weekend.

/3

Direct speech and reported speech in context

Extract from an article 'Farmers using medieval methods to combat rural crime' by Haroon Siddique, *The Guardian*, 6 August 2018

The following text is taken from a news report about rural (countryside) crime and the actions farmers are taking to protect their farms.

Tim Price, the rural affairs specialist at NFU Mutual, said: "There's no doubt that rural crime has changed massively in the last decade.

"Ten years ago it was largely unstructured, stealing from the next village, trying to sell it at a car boot sale. Now we are seeing organised criminals who have

5   links to drugs and the **county lines issues**, **money laundering**, even in some cases, **human trafficking**."

In an attempt to frustrate the criminals, farmers are incorporating medieval measures into their security, according to the 19th Rural Crime report. It says farmers are putting up earth banks and dry ditches to block criminals who use

10   4 x 4 vehicles to get on to farm land.

In Kent, one farmer has spent 18 months surrounding his 4,500 acres with ditches and barriers to deter criminals from **hare coursing** and **fly-tipping**.

Others are using animals including geese, llamas and dogs as a low-tech alarm system, much as landowners did hundreds of years ago. [...]

15   Price said that as thieves had become more sophisticated, police forces had reduced resources because of budget cuts.

The impact, he said, was not just the cost, which can be recovered by insurance, but disruption to farmers' work and fear of being targeted again.

"The knowledge that people are hanging about watching homes and farms, what

20   machinery they've got, that really does cause a lot of worry [among farmers]," said Price.

"We've had cases where people have decided to stop using livestock or stop use of fields because the mental anxiety someone will target them is so great."

county lines issues problems caused by criminal gangs operating outside their usual urban locations

money laundering making money that is gained illegally appear to come from a legitimate (legal) business

human trafficking illegally transporting people for financial gain

hare coursing the illegal activity of hunting hares

fly-tipping illegally dumping rubbish

✎ Activity 1   Understanding the text

a) Circle the correct meaning of the word 'measures' (line 8) in this context.

   finds the size of something   actions taken to achieve a purpose

b) What methods are farmers using to protect their property from thieves?

----

c) What has happened to police resources?

✎ Activity 2   Exploring the writer's technique

a) This text includes Tim Price's words conveyed as direct speech. Why do you think the reporter quotes him directly at these points in the text? Tick the statement below that you agree with most and explain your choice.

  ☐ Readers often focus on the beginning and end of a text.

  ☐ He is the expert and so his own words are important.

  ☐ The words in direct speech make his most important points.

----

b) Find all instances in the extract opposite where the writer uses the word 'said' or 'says'. On separate paper, choose a word from the list below to replace 'said' or 'says' in each case.

   added   pointed out   argued   states   explained

c) Select one paragraph that includes reported speech and explain why you think that the reporter chose to use this rather than direct speech.

✎ Activity 3   Try it yourself

On separate paper, write a short report about something that concerns your class, for example the need to raise funds for a local charity. Include direct and reported speech. You might begin like this:

A local charity has claimed that it urgently needs more funding to support people with disabilities in our neighbourhood.

1 How to improve your spelling

Different people learn in different ways. Try out some of the learning strategies below to find out which helps you best to improve your spelling.

Mnemonics

A mnemonic is a verse or saying that helps you to remember something.

Here are some examples that people use to help them spell particular words.

> **Occasion** – **o**ld **c**ute **c**ats **a**ll **s**leep **i**f **o**ffered **n**ourishment.

> A**ccomm**odation offers **c**omplete **c**omfort in a **m**odern **m**ansion.

> Only a **finite** number of people can spell 'de**finite**'.

✏ Activity 1

Write down a word that you struggle to spell. Then make up a mnemonic to help you remember the tricky part of the spelling. If your mnemonic is funny or means something special to you, it will help you to remember it.

Word   Mnemonic

------------   --

/2

Learn the tricky bit

There is often just one tricky part of a word to spell. If this is the case, write out the word and underline the part that you can't remember. Decide how best to learn this tricky part. Some options are:

- Repeat the tricky letters by chanting them or writing them out many times. For example, for 'argument' try chanting a…r…g…u…m…

- Try to find an image that will help you to remember the tricky part. For example, draw an iron above the word 'env**iron**ment'.

Don't forget the **iron** that is in the env**iron**ment.

Activity 2

On separate paper, write down a word that you find tricky to spell (nouns work particularly well with this strategy). Think carefully about the tricky part of the spelling and then draw a picture with a feature that will help you to remember it.

/3

Recognise prefixes and suffixes

Many words are constructed (built up) from root words and prefixes or suffixes. If you can recognise these different parts in a word, it will help you to spell it.

For example, a common mistake is to spell 'disappear' as 'dissappear'. However, if you can recognise the prefix 'dis', which means reversal, then it is easy to see that it is simply added to the word 'appear', to make 'disappear'. The spelling of a prefix or suffix rarely changes.

Activity 3

Underline the correct spelling of these words and circle the prefix or suffix.

a) dissappoint / disappoint

b) wonderful / wonderfull

c) hopeless / hopeless

d) supaman / superman

/8

Tip

Some people find spelling extremely difficult. Don't despair though! Set yourself a target of learning five spellings per week. These could be from any subject, not just English.

Learn word families

Many words belong to a 'family' that contains other words that are related to each other by meaning, grammar and spelling. If you know how to spell one word in that family, it will help you to spell other words in the same family. Here are some word families below:

person   impersonal   personality   impersonator

danger   dangerous   dangerously   endangered

2 Plurals

What are plurals?

Plural means more than one. It is the opposite of singular.

Most words are different in the plural and singular, although some are the same in both:

| sheep | deer | moose |

Some other words are always plural and have no singular form:

| scissors | trousers | clothes |

How are they formed?

Most plural nouns are made by adding **–s** to the singular noun.

tree ➔ tree**s**

If the noun ends in **–y**, we change the **y** into an **i** and add **–es**. But if there is a vowel (a, e, i, o, u) before the **y**, just add an **s**.

daisy ➔ dais**ies**
journey ➔ journey**s**

Most nouns ending in **–s**, **–ss**, **–x**, **–ch**, **–sh**, **–z** and **–o** add **–es** to make the plural:

bus ➔ bus**es**
tomato ➔ tomato**es**

If the noun ends in **–f** or **–fe**, it can change to **–ves** in the plural form.

hoof ➔ hoo**ves**
life ➔ li**ves**

Find out more

There is more about nouns on page 4.

Tip

There are exceptions with nouns ending in **o**.

photo ➔ photo**s**
video ➔ video**s**

✏ Activity 1

Change the singular nouns into plurals in the story below.

The family __families__ said goodbye, loaded the box _____ on to the cart, and began their

journey. "Don't forget the photo _____," shouted the person _____ who opened the gate.

They continued until they reached an inn, where they took some refreshment. The waiter _____

brought them fresh potato _____ and tomato _____. Unfortunately, the blunt knife

_____ meant that they had to eat everything with their fingers.

/7

(3) Silent letters

What are silent letters?

Some words contain silent letters, which we no longer pronounce.
For example:

> **k**nock   s**w**ord   de**b**t   ans**w**er   We**d**nesday   fas**c**inate   cas**t**le

Some silent letters would have been pronounced in the Middle Ages.

One way to remember these spellings is to say the silent letters to yourself.
For example, say 'Wed–nes–day' when trying to spell 'Wednesday'.

Silent 'e'

Another silent letter is the 'e' at the end of many words. We don't pronounce
it, but it can turn a short vowel sound into a long vowel sound. For example:

> tap ➜ tap**e**   tub ➜ tub**e**   cub ➜ cub**e**

Silent 'h'

Some words start with a silent 'h'.

> **h**onour   **h**our   **h**eir   **h**onest

✏ Activity 1

a) Circle the silent letters in the words below.

doubt   pane   calm   column   design   foreign   ghost

half   listen   plumber   receipt   resign   wrench   heiress   rhino

b) Write five more words that contain silent letters and circle them.

/20

4 Double consonants

What are double consonants?

A consonant is a letter which is not a vowel. These are consonants:

b c d f g h j k l m n p q r s t v w x y z

Some root words double their consonants when they change form, for example when a suffix is added.

How do they work?

Verbs that end in a single vowel (**a**, **e**, **i**, **o** or **u**) and a single consonant (such as **n** in 'run') usually double the final consonant when we add the suffix **–ing** or **–ed**:

> clap → cla**pp**ing → cla**pp**ed
>
> rot → ro**tt**ing → ro**tt**ed
>
> travel → trave**ll**ing → trave**ll**ed

The same rule applies when we add the suffix **–er** to turn the word into a noun.

> run → ru**nn**er   shop → sho**pp**er   travel → trave**ll**er

If the verb ends in a **w**, **x** or **y**, the doubling rule does not apply.

> pra**y** → pra**y**er   ro**w** → ro**w**er   bo**x** → bo**x**er

Tip

There are exceptions to this rule. For example:

> develo**p** →
>
> develo**p**ing →
>
> develo**p**ed

✏ Activity 1

Add a suffix from the list below to each root word and write the new word. Use each suffix twice. Remember that not all of these suffixes will work with these root words. Think carefully about whether you need to double the consonants.

–ed   –ing   –er

a) mix   -------------------

b) chop   -------------------

c) say   -------------------

d) draw   -------------------

e) sit   -------------------

f) develop   -------------------

/6

5 Endings –le, –el, –al and –il

What are the endings –le, –el, –al and –il?

Many words end with the 'l' sound, but this sound can be spelled in different ways: **–le**, **–el**, **–al** or **–il**. It is often tricky to know which spelling is correct.

How do they work?

The ending **–le** is the most common spelling for this sound at the end of words.

table   middle   candle   bottle

The ending **–el** is used mainly after the letters **m**, **n**, **r**, **v**, **w**, **s** and after a soft 'c' or 'g' sound.

camel   tunnel   squirrel   travel   towel   tinsel   parcel   angel

The ending **–al** is often used after the letters **d**, **b** or **t**.

medal   cymbal   capital

There are not many words ending **–il,** so it is best to learn those that do.

nostril   pencil   fossil   stencil   pupil   April   tranquil   peril

Activity 1

A spelling error is highlighted in each sentence below. Cross out the error and write the correct spelling above it. The first one has been done for you.

a) ~~Apral~~ *April* is the cruellest month.

b) He sipped the herbil tea and grimaced.

c) The game was a totel wipe out.

d) The mackeral had bright eyes and shiny scales.

e) Littel specks of dust remained on the trophy.

f) Most people felt the new technology was a marval.

/5

6 Tricky letter groups

Some spellings in English are undoubtedly tricky. This is partly because some letters and letter groups can represent many different sounds.

–ture, –cher and –sure

These three letter groups are easily confused. To determine which ending a word should have, it is helpful to think about the sound, as that will help you pick the correct spelling.

The **–ture** and **–cher** letter groups make the same 'ch' sound. Here are some examples.

> fu**ture**   but**cher**   adven**ture**   vou**cher**

However, the **–sure** letter group makes more of a 'sh' sound. Here are some examples.

> cen**sure**   lei**sure**   mea**sure**   trea**sure**

ie or ei

The **ie** and **ei** letter groups both make the same 'ee' sound. Here are examples of these words.

> f**ie**ld   bel**ie**ve   rec**ei**ve   c**ei**ling

In general, the rule is that 'i comes before e, except after c'.

However, there are exceptions to this rule that you need to learn. If the letter pairs don't make the 'ee' sound or if there is no 'c', the spelling will be 'ei'. Here are some examples of these words.

> w**ei**gh   h**ei**ght   w**ei**rd

> **Tip**
>
> Say the words aloud carefully and listen to the slightly different sound.

Activity 1

Read the sentences below and add the correct letter groups to some of the words. It may be helpful to speak the sentence out loud. Remember that some sounds can be made by more than one letter group.

a) I have always wanted to study Agricul_____ at university.

b) Her leg had a bone frac_____ that needed an x-ray.

c) They were all under pres_____ to meet the deadline.

d) My bike tyre had a big punc_____

e) The prea_____ spoke in front of a large group of people.

/5

Activity 2

Re-read the rules opposite about 'ie and ei'. Look at the words below and circle any that do not follow the rule 'i before e except after c'.

seize   conceited   pie   weird   eight

protein   caffeine   deceit   ceiling   believe

/5

Activity 3

a) Read the paragraph below. Circle any examples of words that have not been spelled correctly.

We climbed the steps and ran through the muddy feild to vencher into the woods. The tempracher was quite hot; in fact, compared to this morning, this afternoon was a scorture! My leg tweaked from my minor leg fracher. To my releif I could still put all my wieght on it, although my teature did say to try not to. We crept through a rusty, wooden gate to reach a small enclocher and realised there was a shortcut home from here. What an advencher!

b) Rewrite this paragraph below, including the correct spellings of the words you have circled.

/20

7 Common spelling mistakes (1)

Some spelling mistakes are made so often that they become familiar and it can be tricky to remember what is correct and what is incorrect. The next couple of units cover some of the most frequent spelling mistakes that students make.

A lot

Some people write 'a lot' as one word – 'alot' – but it should always be separated out as two words.

> There were **a lot** of choices to be made.

Tip

'A lot' (two words) is not to be confused with the verb 'to allot' (notice the double 'l'), which means to distribute or to give out.

Lose or loose?

Some students confuse **lose** and **loose**.

The verb **lose** means become unable to find something.

> I always **lose** my glasses at work.

The word **loose** can describe something that is not firmly fixed.

> The nail was **loose** so the picture fell down.

Program or programme?

The spelling **program** is used for anything to do with computers:

> The Evil Genius had to **program** the computer to download his 'world domination' **program**.

program used as a verb

program used as a noun

The spelling **programme** is used to describe a planned series of events, a booklet giving details of events or a type of broadcast.

> The **programme** said there would be an interval of 20 minutes.

Tip

'Program' is the American spelling of the word 'programme'. It is used in computing because of the American domination of the computer market.

–ce or –se endings?

There is often confusion with words that sound the same but have slightly different spellings.

> advi**se** / advi**ce**   practi**se** / practi**ce**   licen**se** / licen**ce**

In general, if the word is a noun, it is likely to end **–ce**.

I must go to piano **practice**. *noun*

If the word is used as a verb it is likely to end **–se**.

I must **practise** the piano. *verb*

There is more about nouns on page 4 and verbs on page 12.

✏ Activity 1

Correct the eight spelling errors in the text below. The first one has been done for you.

A lot
~~Alot~~ of people loose interest when told to write about their favourite television program. My dad refuses to pay for a TV license which means it's illegal to watch BBC programmes! I tell Dad off about this and advice him to get one as soon as possible. It's poor practise to avoid the license fee because the BBC needs money to fund new programs.

/7

✏ Activity 2

Circle the correct bold words to complete each sentence below.

a) If you **practice / practise** every day, you'll soon be able to walk across this tightrope.

b) Use that **device / devise** to browse the Internet.

c) His tie was **lose / loose** and he was told to do it up properly.

d) You've not made **a lot / alot** of progress in unravelling the mystery.

e) My sister earned a fortune from writing a brilliant computer **program / programme**.

/5

Is my tie **lose** or **loose**?

✏ Activity 3

Write two sentences. The first should use the word 'advice' (as a noun). The second should use the word 'advise' (as a verb).

a) --

b) --

/2

8 Common spelling mistakes (2)

Homophones and near homophones

Homophones are words that sound the same but have different meanings and spellings. Homophones can be confused, so it is important to understand the differences. Some examples are explored below.

Witch or which?

People sometimes choose the wrong homophone and end up spelling the word they intended to use incorrectly.

Witch is a noun that refers to a fictional, supernatural creature.

> The **witch** cackled.

Which is a relative pronoun used to refer to something previously mentioned or an interrogative pronoun used to ask for more information.

> **Which** pencil case belongs to you?

Who's or whose?

Who's is short for 'who is' or 'who has' (the apostrophe shows there are letters missing).

> **Who's** cooking lunch today?   short for 'who is'

Whose is a relative pronoun.

> That is the boy **whose** alligator ate my shoes.   relative pronoun meaning belonging to the person just mentioned

Where, were or we're?

Where, **were** and **we're** sound similar and are 'near homophones'.

Where refers to a place, position or direction.

> **Where** is the railway station?

Were is the simple past tense of the verb 'to be' and is used with the pronouns you, we and they.

> We **were** having a picnic when the wasps came.

Tip

Note that a few words may be homophones in some accents but not in others. For example, in many English accents **paws**, **pours** and **pause** are all homophones, but in Scottish accents, they are all pronounced differently.

Which witch has the cat and **which witch** has the broomstick?

We're is short for 'we are' (the apostrophe shows a missing letter).

We're going to learn how to fly.

You're or your?

You're is short for 'you are' (the apostrophe shows the 'a' has been missed out).

You're never going to tell him, are you?

Your is a possessive determiner.

Eat **your** cabbage.

✏ Activity 1

Circle the correct homophones in the text below.

The **witch** / **which** couldn't decide **witch** / **which** cat to take to the party. She eventually chose the cat **who's** / **whose** fur was shortest and least likely to make her sneeze.

"Come on, jump up," she called. "**We're** / **were** / **where** off for one final attempt. There's no point in looking so sleepy. You need all **you're** / **your** wits about you for this escapade."

/5

✏ Activity 2

Circle the four spelling mistakes in the text below. Write the correct spelling next to each error.

Devesham Dramatic Society presents

The Which's Cauldron

A new play by Emily Middleton
(author of *Whose Afraid of the Big Bad Wolf?*)

Thursday 21st – Saturday 23rd November
Tickets: £5 adults, £3.50 children

Special Offer! Half-price tickets for you're family if you book before
1st November.
Were donating all profits to local charities.

/4

1 Standard and non-standard English

What are Standard and non-standard English?

Standard English is the form of English language that is widely accepted as the correct form for use in schools, in news reports and in formal written documents. It is used as a major world language, both in speaking and writing. You will be expected to write Standard English in most of your essays at school.

Non-standard English has many variations and is spoken more often than written. It includes slang, local dialects and colloquialisms.

How do they work?

To understand exactly what Standard and non-standard English mean, we need to look at a few other terms.

Accent

An accent refers to the way we pronounce (say) words. This depends on where you live. Someone from Dorset will speak English with a different accent from someone from Newcastle, for example. Standard English can be spoken in any accent.

Dialect

Dialect refers to vocabulary (the choice of words), pronunciation and grammar, which may be a result of where you live. For example: a 'sandwich' may be called a 'sarnie' in Sussex and a 'buttie' in Lancashire. One person might say, "I haven't done any homework at all," but in a cockney dialect, another person might include a contraction and a double negative, for example, "I ain't done no homework."

Standard English is a dialect spoken in all of the United Kingdom. A local dialect is spoken by a smaller group of people in a specific geographical area. Local dialect is a form of non-standard English. Many people speak both a local dialect and Standard English, switching between them as necessary (often using non-standard English in speech and Standard English in writing).

Slang

Slang is a very informal style of English, usually spoken rather than written. It refers to non-standard words and phrases. Slang changes all the time and can be influenced by films, television programmes, song lyrics and other media. Slang is an example of non-standard English.

A summary of Standard English:

- It is always used in formal written and spoken English, and sometimes used in informal English.

- It refers to grammar and vocabulary, not accent.

- It is used internationally.

- It excludes local dialect, slang and colloquial words.

Find out more

There is more about formal and informal English on page 80.

✏ Activity 1

Read the statements below and decide whether they are true or false. Tick the correct answer.

	True	False
a) Standard English refers to grammar and vocabulary, not accent.		
b) Standard English can be spoken in any accent.		
c) Social media postings are usually written in Standard English.		
d) Meetings between governments on an international level will usually be conducted in informal English and slang.		
e) You should always write English essays in your local dialect.		

/5

✏ Activity 2

The following sentences are all written in non-standard English. Rewrite them in Standard English.

a) Whadda yer mean?

----

b) I ain't doing my homework.

----

c) That T-shirt is way cool.

/3

Standard and non-standard English in context

Extract from *Tess of the D'Urbervilles* by Thomas Hardy, published 1892

In this extract from the novel, Mr and Mrs Durbeyfield, who are poor, working-class people, have come to believe that they are related to a very wealthy aristocratic family. John Durbeyfield has gone to a local inn to consider his situation.

Mrs Durbeyfield was welcomed with glances and nods by the remainder of the **conclave**, and turned to where her husband sat. He was humming absently to himself in a low tone: "I be – as good as – some folk here and there! I've got a great family **vault** at Kingsbere-sub-Greenhill, and finer skillentons than any man – in
5 **Wessex**!"

"I've something to tell 'ee that's come into my head about that – a grand projick!" whispered his cheerful wife. "Here, John, don't 'ee see me?" She nudged him while he, looking through her as through a window-pane, went on with his **recitative**.

"Hush! Don't 'ee sing so loud, my good man," said the landlady; "in case any member
10 of the gover'ment should be passing, and take away my licends."

"He's told 'ee what's happened to us, I suppose?" asked Mrs Durbeyfield.

"Yes – in a way. D'**ye** think there's any money hanging by it?"

"Ah, that's the secret," said Joan Durbeyfield **sagely**. "However, 'tis well to be **kin** to a coach, even if you don't ride in 'en." She dropped her public voice and continued
15 in a low tone to her husband: "I've been thinking, since you brought the news, that there's a great rich lady out by Trantridge, on the edge o' The Chase, of the name of d'Urberville."

"Hey – what's that?" said Sir John.

She repeated the information. "That lady must be our relation," she said; "and my
20 projick is to send **Tess** to claim kin."

conclave gathering of people	**ye** archaic form of 'you'
vault burial chamber	**sagely** wisely
Wessex an old county in the south of England	**kin** related to / family
recitative speech	**Tess** the Durbeyfields' daughter

✏ Activity 1 — Understanding the text

a) What is John Durbeyfield doing when his wife arrives?

----

b) What is the landlady of the inn worried about?

----

c) Circle the correct meaning of the word 'coach' in this context:

| to train | a carriage drawn by horses | a person who teaches others |

✏ Activity 2 — Exploring the writer's technique

a) The writer uses the phrases below, which are grammatically non-standard.
Rewrite them using Standard English.

I be – as good as… (line 3)

'tis well to be kin to a coach, even if you don't ride in 'en. (lines 13–14)

----

b) The characters use some Standard English and some non-standard English.
  i. Complete the table below with examples of each.

Standard English phrases	Non-standard English phrases
that's the secret	I be as good as some folk

  ii. How do you think this combination of Standard and non-standard English helps
  to convey the characters? Think about how realistic it makes them seem.

✏ Activity 3 — Try it yourself

On a separate piece of paper, write a short piece of dialogue between
two characters about winning the lottery. Include some non-standard
English, such as dialect words and slang. Remember to use speech
punctuation correctly.

Find out more

There is more
about speech
punctuation on
page 60.

2 Formal and informal language

What are formal language and informal language?

Both formal and informal language are types of register. The register of language depends on the audience (who is reading or listening) and the purpose of the speech or writing.

Formal language

Formal language is used with people we don't know well and for serious circumstances and purposes. It can be written or spoken and generally conveys respect for the people you are communicating with. It is used at formal occasions such as interviews, parent–teacher meetings, job applications, government speeches, instruction manuals, essays and legal reports.

Remember: formal language for a formal occasion!

Informal language

Informal language is used with people we know well, on more relaxed occasions. It can be spoken or written. It is used between friends and relatives, on social media, in emails to friends, in speech or dialogue in a story.

How do they work?

Formal language is closely related to Standard English. Some key features of formal language are:

- using words in full rather than contractions ('will not' rather than 'won't')
- using very precise, clear, often technical, vocabulary
- using full sentence structures
- using correct spelling and punctuation.

Informal language may contain some of the following features:

- slang
- contractions ('didn't' rather than 'did not')
- emoticons and emojis (☹)
- overuse of exclamation marks
- question tags (such as 'have you?', 'don't you?' at the end of sentences)
- sentence fragments
- random capitals for emphasis.

Find out more

There is more about Standard English on page 76.

Activity 1

The letter below is written in informal language to a football coach. It contains many informal features, some of which are listed below.

a) Identify and match these features in the text. The first one has been done for you.

informal address

colloquial greeting

incorrect grammar (wrong pronouns)

slang

contraction

question tag

random capitals

overuse of exclamation marks

exaggeration

Hi Mrs Keane

How you doin? Me and my mates want to play footie on the school field on Saturday, you know? We reckon you'd be OK with that as no one uses it then anyway. A million THANKS!!

Laters!

Kaitlin and Ashleigh Paisley

b) Rewrite the letter in appropriate formal language on a separate piece of paper.

/12

Activity 2

The letter below is written in formal language. Rewrite it in informal language, using a style and vocabulary that could be used for a different audience.

Dear Mikaela,

I am writing to thank you for your incredibly generous gift of a cricket bat for my birthday. It was really kind of you to remember me. I know I will get so much enjoyment out of playing with it as the weather gets warmer and the cricket season begins. I am taking part in one of the summer competitions in May with Christopher, Nathaniel and their team, so will let you know the result.

Once again, thank you very much.

Yours sincerely,
Isobel

Here is a sentence you could use to begin your writing.

Hi Mikaela!

Thanks so much for the birthday present. A cricket bat!

/8

Informal language in context

Extract from a social and fashion discussion website

The following text is from a website giving advice about how to deal with difficult or unwanted text messages.

Text: Your parents want to know what on earth happened in the garage and they've left three voicemails.

Answer: Call them, but read from this script. Do not **detract**. Agree with whatever they say. Let them get their anger out at the fact that you spray-painted the inside
5 of their garage rose gold by accident during a DIY Pinterest project gone wrong. "Mom, Dad. I am so sorry. I take full responsibility for what happened in the garage and I apologise for the fact that our garage is now rose gold. It was an accident during a DIY Pinterest project. I was making you a Parents of the Year gift since I know how hard you work, and I saw this really cool trophy that I wanted to give
10 you but it didn't match the decor, and just this once I wanted to do something really *meaningful*, you know?"

So it's a little **manipulative**. It's honest in many ways, too. You are sorry!

Text: Someone wants to know the best time for them to call and you don't want to have the call.
15 **Answer**: "Email is the best way to reach me!"

Add that exclamation for friendliness because a **period** following that shut down is a little scary.

Text: Group chat keeps hounding you for not participating.
Answer: Google the lyrics of your favorite artist or movie and randomly sprinkle
20 throughout the week. One every two/three days should keep you alive.

detract take away part of something

period US term for full stop

manipulative controlling or influencing someone cleverly

✏ **Activity 1**   **Understanding the text**

a) What advice does the writer give about reacting to parents who are angry?

----

b) What does the writer recommend if you don't want to receive a call?

----

c) What form of punctuation does the writer suggest using in order to sound more friendly?

----

d) What does the writer suggest posting on a group chat, and why?

✎ Activity 2   Exploring the writer's technique

a) Look at the vocabulary listed below, which is used in the extract. For each term, explain its formal and informal meaning.

Vocabulary	Informal meaning	Formal meaning
cool		
shut down		

b) Find two other examples of informal language in the text and comment on their effect.

----

c) Why is the first part of the script (lines 6–9) up to '…how hard you work,' suggested by the writer to be read out to parents, presented formally? Think about the effect this might have on the parents hearing it.

----

d) Why does the language become less formal in the second half of the script (lines 9–11)?

----

e) In response to the text about group chats (line 18), the writer uses exaggeration. How does this help to convey an informal tone?

✎ Activity 3   Try it yourself

On a separate piece of paper, write an article for younger children that uses both formal and informal language. You could choose a subject like avoiding too much screen time.

3 Narrative voice

What is narrative voice?

The 'narrative voice' refers to the way a story is told. It may be told by one of the characters or by someone outside the story. Different narrative voices convey different viewpoints and they affect how the reader learns about events in the story.

How does it work?

First-person narrative voice

A first-person narrator tells the story from the viewpoint of one of the characters and uses the first-person pronouns **I** and **we**.

> **I** wandered quietly by the docks, feeling cold and damp. The last time **I'd** been there was with my dad and **we** had been planning our next move.

An advantage of a first-person narrative is that it helps the reader to get to know the lead character and to feel close to them.

A disadvantage of a first-person narrative is that the writer can only write about what the lead character thinks and experiences. That character can't see into the minds of other characters.

Second-person narrative voice

A second-person narrative voice is rare. It places the reader as a character in the story and uses the pronoun **you**.

> **You** wander quietly by the docks.

Third-person narrative voice

A third-person narrator is outside the story and has an overview of all events. This narrator can go inside the mind of any character and often uses the pronouns **he**, **she** or **they**.

> The man wandered quietly by the docks, feeling cold and damp. The last time **he'd** been there was with his father and **they** had been planning their next move.

Activity 1

Read the extracts below and tick what type of narrative voice is used.

Extracts	Narrative voice		
	First person	Second person	Third person
a) I came to the end of the alley and stopped dead.			
b) She looked at Barry and wondered what he was thinking. Barry was just hoping that she would pass the sandwiches.			
c) We were trapped. I whirled round quickly, the wall now behind me, and faced my adversary.			
d) You quickly insert the tracer into the field interface stabiliser and hope that the matter transporter will dematerialise you.			
e) Dickens wanted to help improve the lot of the poor. He wrote with rage against the selfishness of those who ignored them.			

/5

Activity 2

Read the following extract from the novel *Great Expectations* by
Charles Dickens (published 1861). The young boy Pip is recounting one
of his earliest memories – an encounter with an escaped prisoner. Decide
whether the statements below are true or false.

"Show us where you live," said the man. "**Pint** out the place!"
I pointed to where our village lay, on the flat in-shore among the alder-trees
and pollards, a mile or more from the church.

The man, after looking at me for a moment, turned me upside down, and
5   emptied my pockets. There was nothing in them but a piece of bread. When
the church came to itself,—for he was so sudden and strong that he made it
go head over heels before me, and I saw the steeple under my feet,—when
the church came to itself, I say, I was seated on a high tombstone, trembling
while he ate the bread ravenously.

pint point

	True	False
a) The story is told by one of the characters.		
b) This is a third-person narrative.		
c) The escaped prisoner is telling the story.		
d) Pip is telling the story.		
e) Telling the story through Pip's eyes allows the reader to share his experiences.		

/5

Narrative voice in context

Extract from 'Samuel Lowgood's Revenge' by Mary E. Braddon, published 1862

In this extract from the opening of a short story, the narrator, Samuel Lowgood, works as a clerk in a shipping office alongside another young man, Christopher Weldon.

From the first to the last we were rivals and enemies. Perhaps it was on my part that the hatred, which eventually became so terrible a passion between us, first arose. Perhaps it was, perhaps it was! At any rate, he always said that it was so. […]

5   He was very handsome. It was hard for a pale-faced, **sallow**-complexioned, hollow-eyed, insignificant lad, as I was, to sit at the same desk with Christopher Weldon, and guess the comparisons that every stranger entering the **counting-house** must involuntarily make, as he looked at us, – if he looked at us, that is to say; and it was difficult not to look at Christopher. Good heavens! I can see him now, seated at the worn, old, battered, ink-stained desk, with all the July sunlight streaming through

10   the dingy office windows, down upon his waving clusters of pale golden hair, with his bright blue eyes looking out, through the smoky panes, at the forests of masts, dangling ropes, and grimy sails, in the dock outside; with one girlish, white hand carelessly thrown upon the desk before him, and the delicate fingers of the other twisted in his flowing curls. He was scarcely one-and-twenty, the spoiled pet of a

15   widowed mother, the orphan son of a naval officer, and the darling idol of half the women in the seaport of Willborough. […]

I, too, was an orphan; but I was doubly an orphan. My father and mother had both died in my infancy.

sallow yellow and unhealthy   **counting-house** a place where accounts were done

✏ Activity 1   Understanding the text

a) How does the narrator feel about Christopher Weldon?

----

b) How does the narrator know Christopher Weldon?

----

c) Describe Weldon's appearance in your own words.

----

d) Circle the correct meaning of the word 'pet' in this context.

   a domestic animal   to caress   a favourite

✏ **Activity 2**   **Exploring the writer's technique**

a) What narrative viewpoint is this story told from? Which word in the first sentence indicates this?

----

b) How does the narrator describe himself? What does this suggest about him?

----

c) Select one phrase from the second paragraph that indicates how much the narrator dislikes Christopher. Explain what it suggests to the reader about both Christopher and the narrator.

----

d) On a separate piece of paper, rewrite the first paragraph using the third-person narrative viewpoint. You could begin your writing using the sentence below.

   From the first to the last **they** were rivals and enemies...

e) How does this change the effect of the opening of this story?

✏ **Activity 3**   **Try it yourself**

Christopher is seen from the narrator's point of view in this extract. What might he really be like? On a separate piece of paper, rewrite this extract from Christopher's viewpoint.

4 Paragraphs and cohesive devices

What are paragraphs and cohesive devices?

A paragraph is a sentence or group of sentences that form a distinct section in a piece of writing. One paragraph usually contains one main idea. Paragraphs help to break up a text to make it easier to read and understand.

Cohesive devices are words that are used to link ideas in a piece of writing. Cohesive devices include:

- conjunctions, such as: **and**, **but**, **because**, **although**

- adverbs and adverbials, such as: **as a result**, **first**, **consequently**, **when**, **finally**.

Cohesive devices are sometimes called connectives.

How do they work?

A new paragraph should begin every time there is a significant change in a text, such as a change of time, a change of place, a new event, a new topic or a new speaker.

Many paragraphs begin with a topic sentence. A topic sentence summarises what the paragraph will be about. The sentences that follow the topic sentence in the paragraph are known as 'body sentences'.

> **Our solar system consists of eight planets and the sun, along with numerous moons, asteroids and comets.** *topic sentence*
>
> The sun's powerful gravity attracts all of the objects in the solar system. As a result, the eight planets, Mercury, Venus, Earth, Mars, Jupiter, Saturn, Uranus and Neptune, orbit the sun, moving in an anti-clockwise direction. This is what gives us seasons on Earth. *body sentences*

Some paragraphs are connected by a link or a transition sentence, which refers back to a previous paragraph or introduces another paragraph. Link/transition sentences can be used to start a new paragraph and often begin with a cohesive device. For example:

conjunction → **Nevertheless, our solar system is just one of many planetary systems within our galaxy.** ← *link/transition sentence*

Tip

A new paragraph is usually punctuated by an indent in the first line or by leaving a line space.

Find out more

There is more about adverbs and adverbials on page 24.

Activity 1

Match the terms below with their correct definitions. One has been done for you.

structure	words or phrases that help to link a text together
topic sentence	a group of sentences about one main idea
cohesive devices	the overall shape of a text, including a beginning, middle and end
conjunction	the first sentence in a paragraph which introduces the main idea
paragraph	a word that joins words, phrases or sentences together

/4

Activity 2

The text below should be divided into three paragraphs.

a) Mark where you think paragraphs 2 and 3 should begin, using a vertical line.

b) Underline the topic sentence that opens each new paragraph.

c) Circle four words or phrases that act as cohesive devices.

The first *Star Wars* film premiered in 1977. It was not expected to be a commercial success. In fact, several companies thought it was too silly and refused to make it. Even some of the cast thought it was too badly written to do well. And yet, when the film finally arrived in the cinema, it was a smash hit. One of the consequences of the success of *Star Wars* was a revival of interest in science-fiction film and television. *Star Trek* had been off our screens for ten years, but returned as a movie in 1979. The makers of *Doctor Who*, meanwhile, despaired when they saw *Star Wars*. As they had a relatively tiny budget, they couldn't hope to match the special effects of *Star Wars*.

/9

Activity 3

On a separate piece of paper, write at least two paragraphs on a subject of your choice. Make sure that there is cohesion in your work by including some of the cohesive devices explored in this unit.

/10

5 Rhetorical devices

What are rhetorical devices?

Rhetorical devices (also known as rhetorical techniques) are ways of speaking or writing that are used to persuade people to feel or to do something.

How do they work?

There are many rhetorical devices, but three of the most commonly used are explained below.

Repetition

Repetition relies on repeating the same word or the same group of words. It is used to emphasise a point, draw attention to something or make something memorable.

repetition of 'honourable' focuses attention on what it really means and questions the quality in Brutus

"And Brutus is an **honourable** man! Is it **honourable** to plot against your friend? Is it **honourable** to stab him in the back? Is it **honourable** to desire his job?"

The rule of three (tricolon)

The rule of three is a structure. It refers to a group of three words or phrases that act as a summary or a short list of examples. Using the rule of three can emphasise a message to the audience. Politicians and advertisers often employ the rule of three to do this.

And when people ask me, "Will you accept the government's plans?" I say to them:

'Never! Never! Never!'

rule of three to reinforce the message

Harrison Chase Hotels:
Convenience, Economy, Comfort

rule of three to sum up the advantages of Harrison Chase Hotels in their slogan

Rhetorical question

A rhetorical question is a question that doesn't require an answer. Instead, it is intended to make the reader or listener think.

Do we really want the rich to get richer and the poor to get poorer? For the gap between the rich and the poor to get bigger and bigger?

Activity 1

Look at the speech below.

> The rest of you: I want you to scatter throughout the city. Speak to the people. Speak to them of democracy, freedom and fairness. Speak to them of justice, peace and plenty. Remind them that they are human beings! And human beings always have to fight for their freedom!

a) Highlight all the examples of repetition in the speech.

b) Underline two examples of the rule of three.

c) How do you think the speaker intends her listeners to feel after hearing her speech?

/10

Activity 2

Rewrite each statement below as a rhetorical question. The first one has been done for you.

a) We don't want any more crime. <u>Do we want any more crime?</u>

b) We won't put up with the disgusting food in the student canteen.

----

c) We don't want our student privileges to be taken away.

/2

Tip

Notice that the statement is negative ('we don't') but the rhetorical question is positive ('do we').

Activity 3

Look at the rhetorical devices used below. What do you think is the intended effect on the audience? Write a sentence explaining your view.

a) Sale! Sale! Sale!

----

b) Do we really want to live in a country where our freedom of speech is ignored?

----

c) And when people ask me what my priorities are as Prime Minister, I say to them: education, transport, the environment.

/3

Rhetorical devices in context

Extract from a speech by J.K. Rowling to Harvard University graduates in 2008

The following extract is taken from a speech to university graduates by J.K. Rowling (author of the Harry Potter books). Here she explains how, when she felt like a complete failure, she managed to turn her life around by writing.

So why do I talk about the benefits of failure? Simply because failure meant a stripping away of the **inessential**. I stopped pretending to myself that I was anything other than what I was, and began to direct all my energy into finishing the only work that mattered to me. Had I really succeeded at anything else, I might never
5   have found the determination to succeed in the one arena I believed I truly belonged. I was set free, because my greatest fear [poverty] had been realised, and I was still alive, and I still had a daughter whom I adored, and I had an old typewriter and a big idea. And so rock bottom became the solid foundation on which I rebuilt my life. […]

Failure gave me an inner security that I had never attained by passing examinations.
10   Failure taught me things about myself that I could have learned no other way. I discovered that I had a strong will, and more discipline than I had suspected; I also found out that I had friends whose value was truly above the price of rubies.

The knowledge that you have emerged wiser and stronger from setbacks means that you are, ever after, secure in your ability to survive. You will never truly know
15   yourself, or the strength of your relationships, until both have been tested by **adversity**. Such knowledge is a true gift, for all that it is painfully won, and it has been worth more than any qualification I ever earned.

inessential what does not matter   **adversity** difficulty or misfortune

✏ Activity 1   Understanding the text

a) What things mattered to Rowling when she hit 'rock bottom'?

----

b) What does Rowling believe about failure?

----

c) Circle the correct meaning of the word 'discipline' in this context.

set of rules   self control   area of study

✏ Activity 2 — Exploring the writer's technique

a) Rowling begins this part of her speech with a rhetorical question. What effect would this question have had on her audience?

----

b) In the second paragraph, Rowling uses the rule of three to emphasise what failure taught her. What were these three things? (Two are about herself; one is about other people.)

----

c) Rowling repeats the word 'failure' four times in this speech. Why does she do this and what effect does it create?

✏ Activity 3 — Try it yourself

Write a short speech of your own persuading your class about something you consider important. You should include:

repetition   rhetorical questions   rule of three

Glossary

adjective a word that describes a person, place or object (nouns and pronouns)

adjective phrase a group of words that acts as an adjective and has an adjective as its head word

adverb a word that gives more detail about a verb, an adjective or another adverb

adverbs of frequency adverbs that say how often something happens, e.g. *sometimes* or *rarely*

adverbs of time adverbs that say when something is taking place, e.g. *tomorrow* or *later*

adverb phrase a group of words that acts as an adverb and has an adverb as its head word

apostrophe for contraction an apostrophe to show that some letters are missing when two words are combined and shortened (contracted), e.g. *don't* or *we're*

apostrophe for possession (or possessive apostrophe) an apostrophe that shows that one thing belongs to another thing or person, e.g. the *boy's* shoes

auxiliary verb a helping verb that comes before the main verb to help express a tense

capital letter an upper case letter, e.g. A, B or C. Lower-case letters are smaller, e.g. a, b or c

clause a group of words that work together as a unit with a verb as its head word

colon a punctuation mark **:** that can be used to introduce a list, examples or explanations

comma a punctuation mark **,** used to separate information. It can separate items in a list, clauses or direct speech from information about the speaker

command a sentence that usually begins with a verb and instructs you to do something

common noun a noun that names a general thing rather than a particular one, e.g. *girl* or *car*

comparative adjective an adjective that compares two things, e.g. she is *happier* than him

complex sentence a sentence that contains one main clause and at least one subordinate clause. The clauses are joined together by subordinating conjunctions. A complex sentence is a type of multi-clause sentence

compound sentence a sentence that is made up of two or more clauses that are equally important and joined together by a coordinating conjunction. A compound sentence is a type of multi-clause sentence

conjunction (or connective) a linking word that joins words, phrases or clauses, e.g. *if*, *but* or *and*

consonant these letters are consonants: b c d f g h j k l m n p q r s t v w x y z

coordinating conjunction a conjunction that joins two parts of a sentence that are of equal weight (they are both full clauses), e.g. *and*, *yet* or *for*

demonstrative determiner a determiner that shows (demonstrates) which item is meant by saying whether it is near or far, e.g. *this* bag or *those* apples

determiner a word that comes before a noun and gives more information about it, such as which one it is, how many there are, where it is and whose it is, e.g. *an*, *that* or *some*

dialogue spoken words between two or more people

direct speech the exact words that someone says. Direct speech uses speech marks (or inverted commas) to mark the beginning and end of the words spoken

exclamation a sentence that expresses emotion such as surprise, enthusiasm or horror

exclamation mark a punctuation mark **!** that is usually placed at the end of a sentence to indicate that the sentence is an exclamation

full stop a punctuation mark **.** used to indicate the end of a sentence, or to show that a word has been shortened or abbreviated

future tense a tense used to describe things that will happen in the future

head word the most important word in a phrase

homophones words that sound the same but have different spellings and meanings, e.g. *bored* and *board*

indirect object a second object in a sentence that is directly affected by the main object, e.g. I gave a toy to my *nephew*

intensifying adverb an adverb that emphasises another adjective or adverb, e.g. *very* slowly

irregular plural noun a plural noun that does not follow any spelling rules and just needs to be learned, e.g. *men* or *mice*

irregular verb a verb that changes in a unique way, not following the usual pattern and often changing the root of the word

list a number of items recorded one after the other

lower-case letters smaller letters, e.g. a, b or c. Upper-case (capital) letters are larger, e.g. A, B or C

main clause a clause that contains a subject and verb, and makes sense on its own

main verb the main verb details the main action, state or feeling

mnemonic a verse or saying that helps to remember something

multi-clause sentence a sentence made up of more than one clause, each with its own verb; they can include two main clauses, or one main clause and one subordinate clause

noun a word used to name a person, place, idea or thing

noun phrase a group of words that acts as a noun and has a noun as its head word

object the object in a sentence is the person, animal or thing that is on the receiving end of the action (having something done to it)

paragraph a sentence or group of sentences on one idea that forms a distinct section in a piece of writing

past tense a tense used to describe things that have already happened

personal pronoun a word that can be used instead of a noun that refers to a person, people or things, e.g. *she, it, his*

phrase a group of words that form a unit; most phrases do not have a verb so they are not full sentences

plural more than one. It is the opposite of singular, which means just one

plural noun a noun that is more than one. Most plural nouns are made by adding –s or –es to the singular noun, e.g. *foxes* or *hats*

possessive determiner a determiner that shows ownership, e.g. *my, your, Jason's*

possessive pronoun a pronoun that refers to things that are owned, e.g. *mine, yours* or *his*

prefix a group of letters placed in front of a root word to add to or change its meaning, e.g. un– or dis–

preposition a word that comes before a noun, pronoun or noun phrase and links it to other words in the sentence. Prepositions tell you about position, direction, timing or another type of link or relationship

prepositional phrase a group of words that acts as a preposition and has a preposition as its head word

present tense a tense used to describe things that are happening now

pronoun a word that can be used instead of a noun

proper noun a noun that names a particular person, place or thing, e.g. *London*, the *Queen*

punctuation the marks, such as full stop or comma, used in writing to separate sentences and their parts, and to make meaning clear

quantifying determiner a determiner that details quantity or number, e.g. *all, many, fewer*

question a sentence that asks something

question mark a punctuation mark **?** that is usually placed at the end of a sentence to indicate that the sentence is a question

regular verb a verb that follows a set pattern, adding different endings, but leaving the root of the word unchanged

root a word in its most basic form, e.g. *look*

semi-colon a punctuation mark **;** that links together two main clauses that are of equal importance but that suggest a contrast or are closely related

sentence a group of words that expresses a complete idea. Sentences usually have a verb and form a statement, question, command or exclamation

silent letter a letter in a word that is not pronounced, e.g. **g** in **g**nat or **k** in **k**night

single-clause sentence a sentence comprised of one main clause. It is also known as a simple sentence

singular just one. It is the opposite of plural, which means more than one

speech marks (or inverted commas) a punctuation mark that goes at the beginning " and end " of spoken words

statement a sentence that tells you something

subject the person, animal or thing in a sentence that is doing or being the verb

subordinate clause a clause that adds information to a main clause but can't work as a sentence on its own

subordinating conjunction these join a less important part of a sentence (subordinate clause) to the most important part of the sentence (main clause), e.g. *because, until, whereas*

suffix a group of letters that can be added to the end of the root form of a word, e.g –ed or –ing

superlative adjective an adjective that compares more than two things, e.g. she is happier than him, but the cat is *happiest* of all

upper-case letters (or capital letters) larger letters, e.g. A, B or C. Lower-case letters are smaller, e.g. a, b or c

verb a word that identifies actions, thoughts, feelings or a state of being

verb tense the three main verb tenses are past tense, present tense and future tense; they explain whether something is happening now, has already happened, or will happen in the future

vowel these letters are vowels: a, e, i, o u

OXFORD
UNIVERSITY PRESS

Great Clarendon Street, Oxford, OX2 6DP, United Kingdom

Oxford University Press is a department of the University of Oxford. It furthers the University's objective of excellence in research, scholarship, and education by publishing worldwide. Oxford is a registered trade mark of Oxford University Press in the UK and in certain other countries

British Library Cataloguing in Publication Data

Data available

ISBN 978-019-842154-2

10 9 8 7 6 5 4 3 2 1

Printed in India by Multivista Global Pvt. Ltd

Acknowledgements

The authors and publisher are grateful for permission to include extracts from the following copyright material:

Charlie Connelly: *Attention All Shipping* (Little, Brown, 2004), copyright © Charlie Connelly 2004, reprinted by permission of Little, Brown Book Group Ltd.

Joanna Moorhead: 'Let's put the brakes on teen drivers and make them wait until they are older', *theguardian.com*, 11 Oct 2013, copyright © Guardian News and Media Ltd 2013, 2018, reprinted by permission of GNM.

Julie Orringer: 'When She Is Old and I Am Famous', from *How to Breathe Underwater and Other Stories* (Knopf, 2003/Viking, 2004), copyright © Julie Orringer 2003, reprinted by permission of Penguin Books Ltd.

RNLI: Beach Safety advice from website, http://www.rnli.orgwww.rnli.org/education, reprinted by permission of the Royal National Lifeboat Institution, Youth Education.

J K Rowling: 'The Fringe Benefits of Failure', Harvard Commencement speech, 5 June 2008, from *Very Good Lives* (Little, Brown, 2015), copyright © J K Rowling 2008, reprinted by permission of The Blair Partnership for the author.

Haroon Siddique: 'Farmers using medieval methods to combat rural crime', *theguardian.com*, 6 Aug 2018, copyright © Guardian News and Media Ltd 2018, reprinted by permission of GNM.

The authors and publisher are grateful for permission to reprint the following copyright images:

Cover: MyImages - Micha/Shutterstock. **p2**, **p61**: Shutterstock.

Illustrations by Jess McGeachin.

We have tried to trace and contact all copyright holders before publication. If notified, the publishers will be pleased to rectify any errors or omissions at the earliest opportunity.